Preparingthe **Honda CR**and**XR** for**Competition** 2nd edition
written and photographed by **by jim gianatsis**

1979 Edition Contents

1980 Supplement   Pages 65-80

New Additions   Pages 81-84

Originally written and published in1979 as the Moto-X Fox Guide to Preparing the CR and XR Honda for Competition 2nd Reprint and Revised Edition 2011 ©Jim Gianatsis Gianatsis Design Associates / FastDates.com Woodland Hills, CA 91364 USA

The Story Of Team Honda
WORKS BIKES AND FACTORY STARS

Honda Motor Company's involvement in dirt bikes, and in particular the sport of motocross, has always been interesting. For a period of close to ten years Honda held the undisputed position as the world's largest motorcycle manufacturer. But during that time between the middle of the 1960s to the middle of the 1970s Honda never seemed to have more than a passing interest in dirt bikes. Much of this probably due to the company's past heritage with roadracing and a deep commitment in four-stroke road bikes. For a company as large as Honda the burgeoning dirt bike market at that time just didn't fit in to projected sales potentials and profit margins.

That isn't to say Honda didn't know what a dirt bike was. Machines like the CL-72 250 Scrambler, followed by SL models like the 350cc four-stroke twins were popular for desert racing and smooth track scrambles. A Bill Bell-built 350cc Honda won the grueling Baja 1000 back in 1968, and Bud Mclane took an SL-350 to the National Enduro Championship in 1970. But then the lighter two-stroke bikes began taking over, and even though Honda countered with their new lineup of XL singles in 1972, the graffiti was already on trackside fencing across America. Highly modified and reframed Bell-built Honda XL singles continued to reap success in long desert races like the Baja 500 and 1000 where four-stroke reliability paid off occassionally, but for the most part the two-strokes were winning everything in sight.

Honda dealers began clamoring for a competitive dirt bike to sell. Honda, itself, still didn't think there was a large enough market for a race bike to be manufactured in any kind of volume which would be profitable for them. Then there was also the problem that it would have to be a two-stroke bike which would be a direct conflict to their four-stroke comm-

With just the addition of Girling shocks, Gary Jones rode a production CR 250 Elsinore to the 1973 AMA 250cc National Championship.

Honda flew over special works CRs(the first RCs) for their first American motocross at Daytona in 1973.

itment. Finally though, public relations and the exploding dirt bike sales of the other Japanese motorcycle manufacturers forced Honda to go motocross racing whether they wanted or not.

Late in 1972 photographs began leaking out of Japan of Honda's new two-stroke prototype 250cc motocross bike. They had the capability to design the world's best motocross bike and it was obvious they had spared no expense in doing so. For a first-time effort the bike was nothing short of perfect. The production CR 250M Elsinores arrived in America at the beginning of the 1973 season and proceeded to knock the entire motocross community on its head. Everything on it was either aluminum (the gas tank, triple clamps, fork sliders, shoulderless rims) where most of the other manufacturers were still using steel for their bikes, and magnesium (engine cases, wheel hubs, carburetor) where the others were using aluminum. It weighed under 210 pounds and the 5-speed piston ported engine was more powerful than what anyone had been used to up until that time in the 250cc class. It was the only bike to buy those first six months in 1973 and dealers couldn't get enough to sell.

Honda was out to bolster its image with the new Elsinores and a factory motocross team seemed to be the best way to do it. As luck would have it the entire Jones family had just been let go from Team Yamaha and Gary Jones, having just won the 250cc National Championship in 1972, was the fastest rider

in America. Honda signed up the entire Jones family, brothers Gary and DeWayne along with father Don Jones who served as team manager, coach, engineer and mechanic. Later in the season they would be joined by Marty Tripes and then Gary Chaplin.

The racing debut of the new Honda motocross team was at Daytona in March when the stadium race was part of the 250cc National Championship that year. Honda wanted to win its first race badly and had two special prototypes for Gary and DeWayne to run. While they stayed together they were the fastest bikes on the track and seemed to accelerate like open class bikes. Luckily they had problems and didn't win the race because in an interview years later, Gary related that when they pulled the cylinders off the bikes for normal maintaince, they found Honda had put a little more capacity into the engines than the AMA would haved liked.

For the remainder of the year the Honda team raced stock Elsinores with the only major modification being the replacement of the stock Showa shocks for better working Girlings. Marty Tripes used his bike to win the Superbowl of Motocross for the second year in a row and Gary gave Honda his second 250cc National Championship. That fall though, the entire Jones family of which Tripes was also considered a part, was given its walking papers. They were proven winners, but Don Jones had a way of doing things which never seemed to agree with big companies like Yamaha and Honda.

3

Gary Chaplin raced a new Honda open class prototype in the 1973 Trans-AMA Series that fall. Engine capacity was believed to be 450cc and the bike seemed to perform fairly well even though there were no high placings. The top European champions like Ake Jonsson, Hakan Andersson and Roger DeCoster had come over in force and their new long suspension travel works Yamahas, Suzukis and Maicos were clearly superior in handling to the short travel Honda.

Honda's second year in motocross would be disappointing for a company which wanted badly to win. Gary Chaplin was the only experienced veteran on a huge rookie team consisting of Gaylon Mosier, Bruce Baron, Rex Staten and Billy Brossi on the big bikes. Grossi looked to be the only rider who was really quick, winning the 250cc National at Hangtown and finishing fifth overall in the 250cc National Championship for 1974. The rest of the team wasn't as impressive, due in part to the bikes which were now clearly a year behind in suspension travel compared to the other factory bikes. The rear shocks were moved forward on the swingarms to give an increase from four to six inches of rear wheel travel on the Hondas, but the factory Yamahas and Suzukis were getting close to eight inches of travel. The 250cc class also contained too many good riders like Jones, Tripes, Ellis, Howerton and Karsmakers, with Kars-

makers dominating the 500cc class as well.

Where Honda did come out on top to prevent 1974 from becoming a total loss was the newley formed 125cc National Championship class consisting of just four races. The new CR 125M Elsinore had just become available that spring and four unknown kids named Marty Smith, Bruce McDougal, Chuck Bower, and Mickey Boone used the new production bikes to take the top four placings in the series against minor opposition.

Sales of the production CR 250M Elsinore began to curtail drasticly. The bike which had been considered the ultimate motocross machine just a year before was left hoplessly outdated by the suspension revolution and the other manufacturers who appeared quickly with long travel bikes. The Honda factory had so much money tied up in production tooling and stockpiles of bikes they decided not to design a new production bike. Consequently, they spent the next four years trying to sell off the outdated Elsinores with nothing more than minor revisions.

The 125cc Elsinore was selling like gangbusters though, thanks to its lightweight and powerful design which proved to be much better than what the competition had to offer. During 1974, 1975, and 1976 it dominated the 125cc class because nobody offered a really good suspension on their bikes, and there were

Gary Chaplin in the 1973 Trans-AMA Series on Honda's first Open class bike the RC 450-73.

a number of aftermarket accessory companies selling nothing but parts to make the CR 125M highly competitive. And of course there was Marty Smith......

Because of his National Championship in the 125cc class Marty was the only rider Honda retained for 1975 from their otherwise lackluster 1974 season. Joining Marty on the now much reduced Honda team was proven winner Pierre Karsmakers, along with two new backup rookies, Rich Eierstedt and Tommy Croft.

1975 was also the year that Honda proved it was serious about winning in American motocross. Not so much because it would help them sell more motocross bikes, because in that area they still felt the potential was limited, but because they felt the publicity and public relations from motocross was good for the Honda image in general. That's why for the next three years they would campaign National and World Championship events without a serious production motocrosser to sell.

The factory bikes Honda introduced in the spring of 1975 were completely changed, all new RC works bikes designed specifically for long suspension travel and painted the now famous Honda red. Only the RC 125-75 bared resemblence to the production CR 125M Elsinore with a similar looking engine. The RC 250-75 and RC 400-75 had their own unique engine designs which proved to be ultimate in simplicity, function and light weight. Such inovations as adjustable outside ignition timing and rearward positioned transmission countershafts for more consistant drive chain tension with long travel suspension were pioneered in the first RCs. These bikes would later be known as the Type Is because of their nearly upright shock positioning on the swingarm compared to the RCs which would follow in 1976 with cantilever positioned rear shocks and be labeled the Type IIs.

There was a lot of secrecy concerning these bikes. The RC-125 had provision on its engine cases for the addition of what may have been a crankshaft fuel injection system. It was also known that the Open class RC was available in various engine capacities ranging from 360,380,400,420,460 and 480cc as the factory and riders experimented with various bore and stroke ratios and displacements.

Marty Smith proved to Honda they had made the right choice in keeping him on the team as he destroyed the 125cc National Championship for the second year in a row, winning every race but one in an expanded series which now included seven events.

Marty rode in other classes as well when the dates weren't conflicting to finish eight overall in both the 250cc National and 500cc National Champion-

Billy Grossi's RC 250-74 was outdated in the suspension department.

ships. Teammate Pierre Karsmakers took his RC works machine to third overall in the 500cc class.

The 1976 racing season saw the emergence of the new Type II RC works bikes, based on the previous year's design but with cantilever rear suspension for more travel. Combined with a new Showa design leading axle front fork the RC 250-76 and RC 400-76 had 11 inches of travel, up from the 9-10 inches of the previous season. In design the new big-bike RCs seemed clearly superior to the rest of the competition. The only problem was it would be one more year before anyone on Team Honda could prove it. Kars-Makers won two 500cc Nationals and one 250cc National with the new Type IIs, but his highest overall finish in either of the series proved to be fourth in the Open class. Croft and Eierstedt fared even worse.

Marty, meanwhile, was trying to do everything he could to try and hold onto his 125cc crown against the threat of Yamaha newcomer Bob Hannah. Bob clearly had the better bike at the beginning of the Nationals with his new OW 26 waterpumper while Marty had to make do with his old short legged Type RC from the previous year until mid-way through the Championship. But by the time the new RC 125-76 Type II arrived for Marty in July, Hannah had nearly clinched the title. Marty felt the pressure on him and rode like crazy the last few races to make up for lost points. The result was that Marty kept crashing on the new bike he wasn't used to and ended up finishing a distant second overall to Hannah without a single win in the eight race Championship. The only bright spot for Marty all year came when he rode his old bike to beat Hannah at the United States 125cc Grand Prix, winning the race for the third consecutive time.

Pierre Karsmakers left Team Honda in 1977 to return to Yamaha, leaving a vacancy for someone in the open class. Marty jumped at the chance to move up after his problems in the 125cc class the year before. Tommy Croft played backup as the two teamsters took their RC 400-77s, now with 12 inches of suspension travel at each end, to first and third place in the 500cc National Championship. Marty was finally back on top again and the RC 400, thanks in part to the development which Karsmakers had put into it, was clearly the best bike in the class.

Things weren't too bad in the 250cc class that year either as Marty took a close second there with the RC 250-77 behind Suzuki's Tony DiStefano. New Honda teammate Jim Pomeroy followed Marty in third overall, while Tommy Croft was fifth.

Honda was concentrating on the 250cc and Open classes because they were just about ready to introduce the new CR 250R Elsinore at the end of the 1977 season and any victories they could garner could certainly give the new production bike which was closely patterned after the RC 250-77 the send off it needed. The new production CR 125R was another year off so Honda just kept its feet slightly

Left: Smith wrapping up the 125cc National Championship on the RC 125-75 in New Orleans in 1975. Below: Smith on the RC 400-75 in the Trans-AMA Series at Livermore. Right: Karsmakers on the RC 250-75 at a National.

wet in the 125cc Naionals with Warren Reid who placed fourth overall with a leftover RC 125-76 Type II model.

1977 was also the first year that Honda seriously campaigned the World Championships. They had flown Marty over for a few 125cc GPs the year before, but this time they had Brad Lackey and Graham Noyce racing the entire 500cc World Championship series. Brad did extremely well in placing third behind Yamaha's Heikki Mikkola and Suzuki's Roger DeCoster.

For the 1978 season Honda brought out an all-new RC 450-78 for Lackey and the other Open class team riders. The idea must have been that a lighter and more powerful bike would help Brad get the job done where the RC 400-77 had failed. But the new RC 450-78 was almost a step backward in that it had slightly shorter suspension, no floating rear brake and and engine with more power than anyone could use. It was certainly a case of not being able to leave well enough alone. Brad was able to use the new bike to move up to second in the World Championship behind Mikkola, but only because DeCoster was having a bad year and Brad himself was a year more experienced. In America both Smith and Croft were having miserable results with the 450cc and ended up making numerous modifications to theirs. Neither of them did well in the 500cc Nationals as Yamaha cleaned house with Rick Burgett and Rex Staten on the impressive new OW 39s. By the Trans-AMA Series that fall, both Marty and Tommy were back on what basically were RC 400-77s. Brad rode only two races of the Trans-AMA with his RC 450-78 and then left the team to join Kawasaki.

That the 1977 model Type II Honda will go down in motocross history as one of the finest bikes ever designed was proven in the 250cc class for 1978 where the bikes remained basically unchanged from the 1977 season and were nearly identical to the newly released CR 250R production bikes. The only difference being the performance of the factory Showa front forks and Fox AirShox on the Team Honda bikes, compared to the not so hot production Showa suspension on the stock CR 250Rs.

More often than not Team Honda riders used the CRs rather than the much more expensive RCs in the Supercross Series and 250cc National races. The only way to tell who was riding a stocker or not was to go up and inspect the frame serial number for the proper CR or RC designation.

Clockwise from bottom left: Lackey's RC 450-78, Smith's RC 125-76 appeared too late to save the title, Croft on the excellent RC 400-76, Noyce on RC 450-78, Croft on RC 450-78, and Lackey on RC 400-77 with Petty No-Dive front brake.

Marty Tripes returned to motocross and Honda in 1978 where right off he used a production CR 250R to win the Daytona Supercross and open up an initial sprong points lead towards the Supercross Championship. Marty effectively slowed down for the last half of the Series and turned the title over to Bob Hannah as Tripes finished second. At the outdoor 250cc Nationals Tripes was just as quick, and at times quicker than Hannah with his exotic OW 38 Yamaha, winning numerous motos. But because Marty missed the first two races of the Championship due to a knee injury and then suffered air filter and swingarm problems, he never won two motos on the same day. Hannah was almost handed the Championship. New Team Honda rider Jimmy Ellis placed a strong second overall in the Championship, posting one National win in the process. Jim Pomeroy finished fifth overall, with both Pomeroy and Ellis riding CRs and RCs and combinations thereof throughout the Nationals as well as earlier in the Supercross Series.

Honda expanded its team in the 125cc class for the 1978 Nationals with the addition of Steve Wise to join Warren Reid. Much of the year they rode minor revised Type IIs which could be classified as RC 125-78s because of suspension and engine improvements from when the bikes were origionally introduced in 1976. Suspension travel was now up to 11 inches at each end. Midway through the season though, they began riding pre-production prototypes of what would become six months later the 1979 production CR 125R. Warren used the bike to win the National in Rhode Island- the only 125cc race Honda would win all year, but they pulled off a number of second and thirds throughout the series.

The unique thing about the CR 125R was the fact it wasn't patterned after an existing works RC like its bigger brother, the CR 250R, had been. Instead, the CR 125R was a completely new design from its 6-speed reed valved engine to the precedent setting frame which was the first to be designed for use with a taller 23 inch front wheel. Whether a 23 inch front wheel works well under all of the conditions encountered in motocross in questionable, but it certainly can prove to be of a slight advantage on extremely rough tracks.

When the 1979 racing season began Honda was on pretty good footing. The RC 450-78 was a somewhat ill-fated machine and wouldn't be seen again, but the remainder of the RC lineup of works bikes were still highly competitive since the suspension revolution had leveled itself out at around 12-13 inches of travel. Honda also had one of the better lineup of production bikes with their CRs and all that was really needed to turn the CRs into works class machinery were better suspensions.

Steve Wise in action on the long-stroke CR 250R-79 Type III at the Houston Supercross.

Opposite page: Pictured here are the three different types of rear suspension systems built by Honda Motor Company of Japan during the 1979 season. All three use the aluminum swingarm which was expected to become a production item in 1979 on the CR 250R2, but never did appear. American Honda has built numerous steel swingarms of their own design at the the race shop in Los Angeles which have also been seen at races. Most of these steel swingarms are of the banana design.

Above: Cliff White models the long-stroke RC 250-79 with twin downtube frame. This engine might be the basis for a future 250/Open class production bike sharing the same cases and lower end.

Below: This twin downtube frame RC 250-79 will probably be the new 1980 production CR 250. Other than the frame, there will be a new center port exhaust cylinder and matching expansion chamber for a slight horsepower increase. Otherwise, most other parts will be interchangable with present CR/RC 250s.

It was obvious with the 1979 Season that the Supercross Series was beginning to play a dominate role in the development of motocross bikes. Team Honda began the year by introducing a special line-up of light weight RC 250s with RC 125 size gas tanks, aluminum swingarms like the RC 450 that didn't use floating rear brakes, and numerous titanium bolts and fittings. The purpose was to strip about 10 pounds off the bikes to get them down to the AMA weight minimum of 196 pounds. Some of the riders like Marty Smith even opted for shorter suspension at 280mm, down from the normal team setting of 300mm (12 inches).

These were single-purpose Supercross lightweights and they performed well in the stadiums, but they obviously weren't suited for rougher outdoor tracks and lacked the fuel capacity for a 45-minute moto. At the Houston Supercross, just one week before the outdoor 250cc Nationals began, Team Honda unveiled an all-new works bike in the hands of Steve Wise to prove they weren't sitting still in development.

The new Honda RC 250-79 had a totallly redesigned chassis labeled AIDD which featured a twin downtube frame for increased strength and rigidity

This aluminum swingarm, with no floating rear brake, but the brake backing plate keyed to a tab on the inside of the swingarm was used on the special lightweight RC 250-79 Supercross bikes. Strangely enough, Graham Noyce used this set-up as well on his RC Grand Prix bike though it couldn't have worked too well on the extremely rough European tracks. For smoother Supercross tracks a full-floating rear brake wasn't important and the non-floater saved weight. This bike is pictured on page 24.

The full-floating rear brake system like this one was popular for the RC bikes used on outdoor tracks where rear braking performance was more important on rougher courses than saving a pound or two. This is Warren Reid's twin front downtube framed RC 250-79 Type III bike. Notice how the brake actuator arm is located ahead of the wheel axle for protection, probably meaning this is a production rear brake with just the addition of a spherical rod end torque arm.

Steve Wise's long-stroke RC 250-79 Type III used a full-floating rear brake as well, but in conjunction with an RC brake backing plate with the actuator arm located behind the axle. Notice how the rear brake pedal is positioned further back on the frame to keep brake rod, torque rod, and axle to swingarm pivot distances equal. The highly-machined aluminum torque arm is very light and very expensive.

over the single front downtubes Honda had used on all their motocross bikes up till then. The aluminum swingarm was designed to work with a full-floating rear brake which was necessary for rougher outdoor tracks. Suspension travel was 300mm at each and provided by Showa spring works forks up front and Fox AirShox at the rear. The new bike remained extremely light at just 200 pounds.

The twin downtube frame allowed the use of a new long stroke ME engine design with center port exhaust on the cylinder. The transmission remained a 5-speed unit, but housed in the smallest and most compact set of engine cases Honda had yet built, and different primary gearing and ratios were used to take best advantage of the new long stroke's broader and stronger low RPM powerband. The bike proved extremely successful on its first outing and Steve Wise placed second both evenings in the Astrodome behind Supercross Champion Bob Hannah. It was hinted that the ME/AIDD bike would serve as a prototype for a new CR 250 production bike to be released in 1980.

England's Graham Noyce, Tuner Bill Buchka, and the Honda RC 450-79 which they raced in the 500cc World Championship.

Team Honda Motocross for 1979 included, from left to right: Warren Reid, Jimmy Ellis, Marty Smith, team manager Gunnar Lindstrom, Marty tripes, Gary Semics and Steve Wise.

No new works bike was planned for introduction in the Open class for the 1979 Nationals, so Marty Smith went to work testing various engine displacements from 360,400cc,450cc,450cc to 493cc fitted into the now conventional Type II style chassis, with certain swingarm and rear frame section modifications. Marty found he could turn 4 seconds a lap faster at Carlsbad Raceway on the easier to ride and lighter 360cc engine bike than with any of the larger engines. This engine is nothing more than an available Mugen kit fitted to a CR/RC 250 lower end similar to the Moto-X Fox Honda of Jim Turner's described in another chapter. There have been reliablity problems with things like kickstarter gears breaking, but Mugen expects to have the problems solved. If not, Marty will then probably go to the first available small displacment works engine which is the 400cc model which took him to his 1977 National Championship.

Team Honda's racing history has shown them to be one of the major inovators in the design of simple, reliable and highly competive motocross machinery. The policy of Honda Motor Company of Japan and American Honda is to compete in National and International motocross racing to help promote the entire line of Honda production bikes. That is why, at times, they do not seemed to be too concerned about selling motocross bikes to the general public. The huge sales of the other motorcycle manufacturers in the motocross market though, is certainly changing Honda's course of thinking in this regard. Soon we may see revised new CR models introduced each season, and perhaps even the addition of an Open class bike to the lineup. But for now we have to take consolation in the fact that when Honda does introduce a new production motocross bike, those bikes have always proven in the past to be better than what any other manufacurer is offering at the time. And thats usually with just the investment in similar quality suspension components as being used by the Honda team it is possible to have a bike which is identical to what the factory Honda riders are riding.

BASIC CR HONDA MODIFICATION ADVICE FROM CLIFF WHITE AND MOTO-X FOX

He is one of the rare breed of factory motocross mechanics. Not the normal mechanic/parts changer that most team manager have to settle for and take satisfaction in knowing that at least the bikes will be maintained in the same condition which they were built. Cliff White is a real tuner. Someone who can take a bike and prepare it to its greatest possible potential. Making that bike work for his rider better than even the factory engineers who designed it ever expected it to. And even then he can go beyond the

origional design when necessary, modifying and changing it with his skill and experience to make it an even better bike. One which will give his rider an advantage that the competition just might deem unfair at times as they follow it across the finish line.

Cliff's rider is Honda star Steve Wise, and Cliff is one of the top tuners with Team Honda. Cliff's experience dates back to when he tuned for Kawasaki's Canadian National Champion, Jan Eric Salqvist, having built a radical long-travel Kawasaki in 1975 that used a Husqvarna 360 CR cylinder assembly mated to the Kawasaki engine's lower end.

During the 1977 season Cliff teamed up with privateer Steve Wise, modifying a Honda CR 125 for Steve that they campiagned on the National circuit. Rebuilt from the ground up, Cliff's Honda out-performed most of the exotic factory bikes and Steve used it to finish as high up as 2nd place in Houston and then 5th overall in the 125cc National Championship. Cliff relied upon Moto-X Fox for the suspension components used on his radical red racer. For the Trans-AMA Series that fall they picked up full support from Moto-X Fox. With Cliff helping on the wrenches, Steve's performance throughout the 1977 season was good enough to garner them a position with Team Honda beginning in 1978.

Being with Team Honda, Cliff has had a lot of experience in testing and preparing the CR 125R and CR 250R production bikes for competition. The team doesn't always race RC prototypes, and quite often they can be found racing production and pre-production CRs in Supercross, Nationals and local events.

Please keep in mind that the changes Cliff suggests are for the more serious Pro-caliber riders and that the production Honda CRs are perfectly adequate in stock form for the majority of riders to which they were sold. Motocross is a highly competitive sport and constantly changing in technology. Because of this improvements can be continously made to any bike, whether it's a production Honda CR, a works Honda RC, or a bike from any other manufacturer. Sometimes sacrifices have to be made in the trans-

Opposite page: Cliff White with the long-stroke RC 250-79 type III Honda. Above: Texas Tornado, Steve Wise. Below: Steve and Cliff compaigned an old style CR 125 which was highly modified and set up with Moto-X Fox suspension parts in the 1977 125cc Nationals to earn a factory ride.

ition of a bike's design from prototype to production form, but only because that production bike has to meet the needs of the majority of riders at a price they are willing to pay. Most riders will never race Nationals nor do they need National caliber equipment. But that also doesn't mean a rider can't benefit from improving his equipment, particularly as that rider's own riding ability increases.

Honda CR125R Elsinore 1979

SPECIFICATIONS:

IMPORTER: American Honda Motor Co.
100 W. Alondra Blvd.
Gardena, California 90247

CATEGORY: motocross

SUGGESTED RETAIL PRICE: NA

ENGINE
Type	two-stroke vertical single
Port arrangement	one reed-valve-controlled intake, four main transfers, one booster, one bridged exhaust
Bore and stroke	56mm x 50.7mm
Displacement	124.9cc
Compression ratio (corrected)	8.4:1
Carburetion	one 32mm Keihin slide/needle
Air filter	two-stage washable oiled foam element
Lubrication	pre-mixed fuel and oil
Starting system	primary kick
Ignition	internal-rotor magneto CDI
Charging system	none

DRIVETRAIN
Primary drive	straight-cut gears
Primary drive ratio	3.15:1
Clutch	wet, multi-plate
Final drive type	#520 chain (⅜-in. pitch, ¼-in. width)
Final drive	13/51: 3.92:1

Gear	Internal gear ratio	Overall gear ratio	MPH per 1000 RPM
I	2.54	31.44	2.4
II	1.87	23.23	3.3
III	1.56	19.28	4.0
IV	1.30	16.11	4.8
V	1.14	14.07	5.5
VI	1.00	12.39	6.2

SUSPENSION/WHEEL TRAVEL, IN.
Front	37mm-diameter stanchion tubes/10.8 in. (274mm)
Rear	Showa gas-charged, 3-way adjustable spring preload/10.6 in. (269mm)

BRAKES
Front	drum, single-leading shoe
Rear	drum, single-leading shoe, rod-operated

TIRES
Front	3.00-23 Bridgestone Motocross-M15
Rear	4.00-18 Bridgestone Motocross-M16

DIMENSIONS AND CAPACITIES
Weight	197 lbs. (89.4 kg)
Weight distribution	47.7% front, 52.3% rear
Wheelbase	56 to 57.1 in. (142.2 to 145cm)
Seat height	37.5 in. (952mm)
Handlebar width	33.5 in. (851mm)
Footpeg height	16.1 in. (409mm)
Ground clearance	14 in. (356mm), at frame
Steering head angle	28 degrees from vertical
Front wheel trail	5.2 in. (133mm)
Frame	tubular chromoly, single front downtube
Fuel tank	aluminum, 1.7 gal. (6.5l), no reserve
Instrumentation	none
Top speed (calculated)	62 mph (99 kph)

All weights and measurements are taken with machine unladen and fuel tank empty.

Showa unreservoired gas-emulsion shocks

PERFORMANCE:

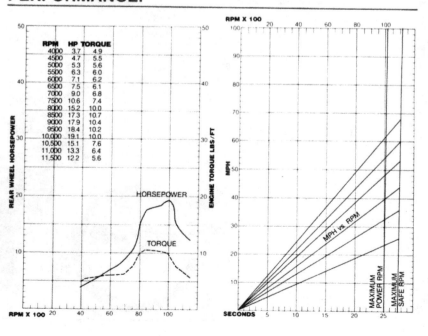

RPM	HP	TORQUE
4000	3.7	4.9
4500	4.7	5.5
5000	5.3	5.6
5500	6.3	6.0
6000	7.1	6.2
6500	7.5	6.1
7000	9.0	6.8
7500	10.6	7.4
8000	15.2	10.0
8500	17.3	10.7
9000	17.9	10.4
9500	18.4	10.2
10,000	19.1	10.0
10,500	15.1	7.6
11,000	13.3	6.4
11,500	12.2	5.6

CR-125R

The 125R powerplant is one which Honda has done a really good job on. It's difficult to make any modifications to it with one exception, as Cliff points out.

"The bike does need more carburetion. The stock 32mm Kehin just isn't enough. A 34mm Mikuni is the hot ticket. It both smooths out the stock powerband and will extend the powerband at top RPMs.

"The engines by themselves, after improving the carburetion, have more than enough steam for the class. No doubt the aftermarket companies will be bringing out hop-up parts for the engine, but there are other areas where it would be wiser to spend your money first."

These other areas include the suspension and beginning at the rear of the bike is the best place to start.

"The CRs really need some good rear shocks. Fox AirShoxs are probably the best. That's what we use on Steve's factoy bikes. The AirShoxs you order off the shelf to fit the CR-125R will probably have the dampening a little too stiff for such a lightweight bike and you will have to change the dampening to something a little softer.

"Along with the shocks, an aluminum swingarm that's well made would both stiffen up the rear end and reduce weight over the stock steel swingarm."

Fox AirShoxs have always been acknowledged as the best rear shocks you can put on a bike, being used by more factory teams including the majority of Team Honda riders for use on both their CR and RC race bikes. Along with the AirShox there are now the new Fox Factory Shocks. These Fox Factory Shocks rival the AirShox in both performance and reliability. The Fox Factory Shock is a new design De-Carbon gas/oil reservoir shock with coil-over two-stage progressive and straight wound springs. Where the Fox Factory Shock differs from the AirShox is that the Fox Factory Shock can be dialed-in once and then left alone, while the AirShox should have its pressures adjusted weekly to tune it for particular track conditions.

The Fox Factory Swingarm is available to provide the CR-125R with either 12-13 inches of rear wheel travel depending upon the length of shock chosen. Made of heat-treated aircraft quality aluminum this swingarm is undoubtably the strongest you can put on a Honda.

"The stock Honda forks may get a little spongy. The springs in the forks seem to go away as soon as you pull the bike out the crate. The forks need a heavier spring, but you can get around the need for different springs by installing air caps. We put air caps on the bikes we use and set the pressures at 3-4 PSI."

The discussion then shifted to any other improvements which could be made to a stock CR-125R.

"A lot of the other stock parts are excellent as the

Light, unusually short six-speed engine

Patented "grid-pattern" reed petals

The CR's multiplex-transfer port system

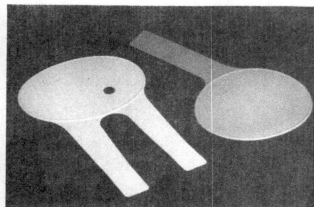

Front number plates with cable guards are important for safety to prevent a snagged cable. A good quality air filter like the Poly-Air will help protect your engine better than the stock Honda filter.

bikes come. Things like the stock wheels, the rims, spokes, hubs are really beefy. The bike already comes with heavy-duty 520 chain and sprockets. You might want to switch to a Gunner Gasser throttle or shorty levers, things to suit your own personal taste, but the standard Honda parts work just fine.

"One thing you will have to change, though, are the stock tires which aren't even good for going slow.

"The only replacement tire available at this time is the Yokohama 23 inch front tire, but it is so thin it's impossible to keep it from flexing. We are still looking for a good replacement tire for the 23 inch front wheel. When Steve Wise runs a Yokohama on a production RC we have to set the air pressures way up to around 16 PSI to gain any handling control because of tire side wall flexing."

Probably the easiest solution to the lack of availability of a good 23 inch front knobby is to change the front wheel assembly to one that's 21 inches. The necessary parts are available from Honda dealers and Moto-X Fox to do it, but this can lead to other problems as Cliff points out.

"The CR-125R had had its frame and suspension geometry designed for a 23 inch front wheel. The bike needs a 21 inch front wheel, but the frame's steering head angle should be moved out some to compensate for the decrease in fork angle which will take place when a change is made to a 21 inch front wheel. Then you need to put on a longer fork to

Honda's Warren Reid and mechanic Brian Lunnis use Fox AirShoxs on their 125cc factory bikes. The rear shocks are the first piece of equipment you'll want to improve on your stock CR 125R.

compensate for the drop in wheel/axle height, which which is 1 inch.

Such a modification is easy for Team Honda to make in their race shop and because they hardly ever race with stock CR forks. Whenever they have raced a CR production bike in the Nationals it has always

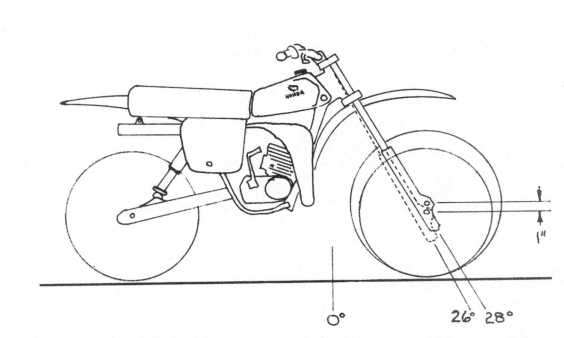

Bolting on a 21-inch front wheel assembly to replace the stock 23-inch wheel assembly which comes on the CR 125R will cause a decrease in steering head angle and make handling dangerous. To make the change to a smaller diameter front wheel you'll need to change to longer travel forks like those from Fox Factory. An increase in fork travel from the stock 274mm to 300mm will regain the needed steering head angle along with a slightly longer wheelbase for additional stability at high speeds.

been equipped with longer RC works forks.

This leaves the privateer with two choices. For local caliber racing on a limited budget it is perfectly satisfactory to stick with the stock 23 inch front wheel assembly and stock forks with added air caps as already mentioned. You'll just have to make do with the presently available Yokohama tire, running slightly higher air pressure than normal to compensate for the tire's light body, and make the switch to a better tire if and when a better tire does become available.

The more serious professional caliber rider will want to make more complex changes to his front suspension as the degree of competition and his riding skill warrants. This centers around a better front fork assembly and Moto-X Fox's new Fox Factory Forks are the best available to the privateer rider with performance to equal or exceed the better factory forks. Fox Factory Forks offer nearly unlimited tuneability as well as being available in 11-inch travel, or in additional 12-inch and 13-inch travel lengths.

For riders wanting to change to a 21-inch front wheel assembly the advantage of longer travel 12-inch Fox Factory Forks over stock Honda forks is important. The additional travel of the Fox Factory Forks helps to compensate for the 1 inch radius change and subsequent dropping of the front end of the bike when changing from a 23-inch to a 21-inch front wheel. Additional fine-tuning of the front geometry is available by the raising or lowering of the fork tubes in the triple clamps. The stock Honda CR forks are not designed to be repositioned in their triple clamps and don't have enough free fork tube on either side of the triple clamps to do so. When changing to a 21-inch front wheel, longer travel Fox Factory Forks allow the switch to be made without having to resort to modifying the frame's steering head angle. And of course there is the gain in front suspension travel without an increase in height at the front of the bike.

1979 Honda CR250R

SPECIFICATIONS:

IMPORTER: American Honda Motor Co.
100 W. Alondra Blvd.
Gardena, California 90247

CATEGORY: motocross

SUGGESTED RETAIL PRICE: $1748

ENGINE

Type	two-stroke vertical single
Valve arrangement	one reed-valve-controlled intake, four transfers, one booster transfer, one exhaust
Bore and stroke	70mm x 64.4mm
Displacement	247.8cc
Compression ratio	7.3:1
Carburetion	one 36mm Keihin slide/needle
Air filter	washable oiled foam element
Lubrication	pre-mixed fuel and oil
Starting system	primary kick
Ignition	flywheel magneto CDI
Charging system	none

DRIVETRAIN

Primary drive	straight-cut gears
Primary drive ratio	3.25:1
Clutch	wet, multi-plate
Final drive type	#525 chain (5/8-in. pitch, 5/16-in. width)
Final drive	14/49:3.5:1

Gear	Internal gear ratio	Overall gear ratio	MPH per 1000 RPM
I	1.90	21.61	3.6
II	1.59	18.09	4.3
III	1.24	14.11	5.5
IV	1.00	11.38	6.8
V	.84	9.56	8.1

SUSPENSION/WHEEL TRAVEL, IN.

Front	37mm stanchion-tube diameter/11.8 in. (300mm)
Rear	3-way adj. spring preload/11.0 in. (280mm)

BRAKES

Front	drum, single-leading shoe
Rear	drum, single-leading shoe, rod-operated

TIRES

Front	3.00x21 Bridgestone Motocross M-15
Rear	5.10x18 Bridgestone Motocross M-16

DIMENSIONS AND CAPACITIES

Weight	220 lbs. (99.8kg)
Weight distribution	45.9% front, 54.1% rear
Wheelbase	56.9 to 58.1 in. (144.5 to 147.5cm)
Seat height	37.3 in. (947mm)
Handlebar width	33.3 in. (846mm)
Footpeg height	15.5 in. (394mm)
Ground clearance	12.3 in. (312mm), at engine cradle
Steering head angle	28.75 degrees from vertical
Front wheel trail	4.65 in. (118mm)
Frame	tubular chromoly steel, single front downtube
Fuel tank	aluminum, 2.4 gal. (9l), no reserve
Instrumentation	none

PERFORMANCE

Top speed (calculated)	69 mph (111 kph)

All weights and measurements are taken with machine unladen and fuel tank empty.

PERFORMANCE:

HONDA CR250R

RPM	HP	TORQUE
3500	7.3	11.0
4000	8.2	10.8
4500	9.2	10.7
5000	11.9	12.5
5500	19.6	18.7
6000	24.7	21.6
6500	25.7	20.8
7000	27.3	20.5
7500	27.7	19.4
8000	27.4	18.0
8500	17.8	11.0

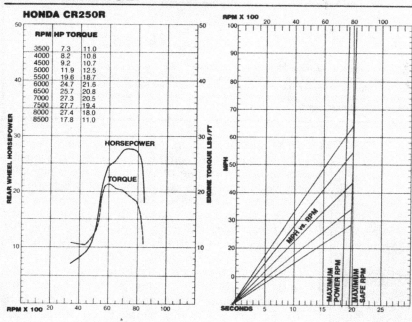

CR-250R

The 250cc Honda motocrosser seems to suffer from the same shortcomings as its littler brother. That is any compromises to be found on the CR 250R are in the stock suspension. It is to Honda's credit that the rest of the bike...the engine and chassis...ranks among the best in its class. The fact that the stock suspension is only marginally adequate is probably Honda's attempt ot hold down the price of the bike for the majority of non-serious riders and racers who buy the bike. Still, other manufacturers do manage to equip their production bikes with good suspension components and still sell the complete bike at a competitive price.

It is interesting to note that Honda has approached Moto-X Fox in the past in regards to having Fox Air-Shox as origional equipment on the CR production bikes. The deal was never able to materialize because Moto-X Fox was unable to provide Honda with the large quanity of AirShoxs they needed and still maintain the quality of the AirShox at the price Honda wanted to pay for them. Obviously though, Honda regards the AirShox as the best rear shock absorber available and the use of the AirShox by the majority of Team Honda riders proves the point.

Cliff points out that the first place to begin improving the CR 250R is in the suspension.

"The 250s need help in the suspension, too. Air caps are needed on the front forks to compensate for the quick sacking out in spring rate of the fork springs. Pressure doesn't need to be very high, just a few PSI to hold the front end up where you want it.

"In back, replacing the stock shocks with AirShoxs is the way to go."

The ultimate performing suspension for the CR R certainly includes a set of gas/spring Fox Factory Forks. They are the strongest, best performing and offer more tuning variations than any other front fork assembly available. Available length of travel are 11, 12, and 13 inches.

Besides the AirShox for the rear suspension, Moto-X Fox now has available the Fox Factory Shock. This is a coil-over shock of the deCarbon type, comp-

letely adjustable for spring rate and dampening, easily rebuildable, and is available with either remote resevoirs or piggyback resevoirs mounted to the main shock body.

Also available is the Fox Factory Swingarm for the CR 250R which is quite a bit stronger and lighter than Honda's stock steel arm. Besides an improvement in handling, straight line tracking is also much better because of the Fox Factory Swingarm's longer length of approximately two more inches. Rear wheel travel can be set at either 12 or 13 inches depending upon choice of shock length.

The engine department of the CR 250R is one place that can be left well enough alone. The Hondas

Marty Tripes' favorite Honda is the CR 250R with improved suspension.

Team Honda brought out special light weight RC factory bikes for the 1979 Supercross Series which weighed right at the FIM's 196 pound minimum. A non-floating rear brake was used to save weight, along with a factory aluminum swingarm. This bike can be duplicated with the similar CR 250R production bike and Moto-X Fox suspension components. Pictured here is Gary Semics' bike with 300mm of suspension travel using Fox AirShoxs and Showa factory forks. A smaller CR 125R style gas tank is also used for shorter Supercross races.

probably have the best engines in the 250cc class with the best powerbands.

"The latest bikes have been coming a little rich in the jetting of their Kehin carburetors. They come with a no. 182 main jet and under normal conditions you can go a little leaner after the engine is broken in. A no. 179 or 180 main jet seems to work well and then lower the needle one notch.."

Check the chapter on carburetion for specific details on how to determine exact carburetor jetting.

Between the 1978 model CR 250R and the 1979 model CR 250R2 Honda made some cylinder porting and reed valve changes which smoothed out the powerband and actually increased low and mid-range power, while raising the CR's claimed peak power output to 37 HP @ 7500 RPM. The older R model engine has a peakier powerband and may, hence, feel faster in seat of the pants riding, but it isn't as easy to control. When you go to replace a worn or broken reed valve assembly or cylinder be sure to order the newer 1979 model R2 parts. The chrome cylinder itself should almost never wear out as long

as you take care to keep it breathing through a good quality and clean air filter such as the type available from Moto-X Fox. If you replace the piston and ring when they show excessive signs of wear, before piston slap damages the chrome cylinder liner plating, the cylinder should last as long as the rest of the bike.

"As far as the rest of the bike, we run all the stock parts," explains Cliff. "Stuff like the wheel assemblies gives us no problems at all. Just be sure to service regularly the things that most people might tend to overlook...like keeping the bushing greased on the floating rear brake arm and the needle bearings in the swingarm pivot."

The CR 250R comes stock with 21-inch and 18-inch wheels, so there is no problem finding a good replacment tire for the "Saddleback Roadrace Specials" that come on the bikes when new. The bike will work well with a 300/350x21 up front and a 450x18 at the rear. Metzeler is the favorite brand of most of the top riders, though Trelleborg and Dunlop offer equally good tire designs, and Yokohama isn't too far off with their usually less expensive designs.

Marty Tripes also favors the conventional CR-type 250 for Supercross races. The only major changes are Showa factory forks, an aluminum swingarm and Fox AirShoxs. Team Honda riders like Warren Reid began using the Fox Factory swingarm when it became available. Below: Marty Smith's 1979 National bike was an RC/CR 250 with a 360cc Mugen kit. Simons front forks were used for part of the series, then Fox Factory Forks.

MOTO-X FOX'S RADICAL CR 250/360 HONDA

Above: Keith Bontrager (left) and Jim Turner (right) with the Moto-X Fox modified CR 250R Honda they raced in the 1979 250cc World Motocross Championship. The bike was originally set up with 330mm (13 inches) of travel the first half of the 1979 season, but it was later reduced to 300mm (12 inches) to suit the the tighter European tracks. The engine was left stock with the exception of later milling the head the thickness of one head gasket to increase compression slightly.

Opposite: Brad Lackey has been intrumental in the development of Fox Factory suspension components like AirShoxs and the origional prototype Fox Factory Forks pictured here. Brad will continue to test and use Moto-X Fox products now that he is riding for Team Kawasaki. No other factory forks, including the exotic Showa and Kayaba works units, can match the performance and strength of Fox Factory forks.

When Honda unleased their long awaited production CR 250R motocrosser at the beginning of 1978 the privateer's dreams were once again answered. Here was one of those rare machines which seldom come out of Japan...a nearly exact copy of the RC 250 works bikes being used by Team Honda riders. Sure there was one major compromise to keep the price down, the performance of the suspension components weren't equal to the high priced forks and shocks on the works bikes, but in 1978 the stock suspension was something you could live with if you had to.

Many times Team Honda riders like Marty Tripes and Marty Smith raced CR production bikes equipped with Fox AirShox and Showa factory forks. Set up like this the CRs are just as competitive as the RC factory machines and the only way to tell the bikes apart was to go up and read the serial numbers on the frames.

With the exception of a few rather minor technical improvements, the production CR 250R2 remains unchanged for the 1979 season. The stock Showa shocks and forks which were adequate the previous

year are now nearly unsuitable for serious professional racing. Honda also failed to equip the new R2 models with an expected lighter and less flexable aluminum swingarm which the factory riders had been running on their bikes in place of the heavy stock steel arm.

Still, the Honda CR 250R,R2 retains the basics to be turned into a top of the line Grand Prix machine thanks to its excellent frame and engine design which are both still years ahead of most other bikes. All the stock Honda needs is a better suspension to remain competitive.

Moto-X Fox has quickly earned a well-deserved reputation as the leader in suspension technology in America. Last year you couldn't put a better suspension system on a Honda CR than Fox's rear suspension kit which consisted of 17.5 inch AirShoxs and an aluminum Thorwaldson swingarm to gain a full 12 inches of rear wheel travel. Up front, 11 or 12 inch travel Simons air/spring forks were the best ticket a privateer rider could buy. A stock Honda set up with just these components carried Jim Turner to the Canadian National Championship during the fall of 1978.

For the 1979 racing season though, Moto-X Fox has introduced a complete new lineup of suspension components under the brand name of Fox Factory. These components were designed at Fox Factory by

Above: Large aluminum accumulator caps on Fox Factory Forks provide the best air/spring rates. Below: Top up and coming privateers like Lenny Giger rely on Fox suspension to build a competitive National bike.

engineers, Bob Fox, Keith Bontrager, Mark Jones and Bob McBroom. Not ordinary kids banging out parts in some garage, mind you, but four college graduate engineers, two of which have backgrounds in the aerospace industry. Their attempt was to design, build, test and produce the finest suspension components that will not just rival, but will out perform the exotic works suspensions on the best Japanese factory team bikes.

Pictured on these pages are Jim Turner and Keith Bontrager with the Fox Factory equipped Moto-X Fox CR Honda which they are compaigning in the 250cc World Championships, selected International races and the final rounds of the American 500cc Nationals for 1979. How in the hell can they race a 250cc Honda in the Open class you ask?. Easy. The bike pictured here also has a production type engine of 360cc to bolt right into the frame. It's the most outrageous production bike that Honda never built, but you can. It's not cheap, but then again, it is a lot less expensive than any factory bike if you could buy one. More about the engine in a moment. First let's look at the suspension.

Probably the most inovative part on Turner's bike is the Fox Factory Fork assembly which is better than any protoype fork assembly being used by the factory teams on their exotic works bikes. The fact that they are available to the privateer at a reasonable price makes them really amazing.

The Fox Factory Forks are the strongest forks ever built. Large diameter 44mm legs of specially heat-treated lightweight thin-wall tubing has less flex, more strength than any fork tubes ever built. The diameter is 2mm larger than the 42mm fork tubes on the factory RC Hondas, previously the strongest forks on a works bike.

Fox Factory Forks also have the first forged aluminum slider legs which provide a significant increase in strength over conventional cast parts. The triple clamps are forged as well, then computer tape milled for precision tolerances and relived for less weight. Handlebars are rubber mounted to help prevent vibration. Fork slider legs are keyed to fit the front brake backing plates of the particular bike application rather then resorting to a torque arm as found on every other type of accessory fork. Steering head bearings are Timken tapered roller assemblies.

Dampening is more refined than on any other production bike. A computer-generated tapered dampening rod design incorporating a unique rebound relief valve never before offered in any production fork is similar to those in the best factory forks.

These forks use combination gas/coil spring suspension with three (3) optional main springs and three (3) optional negative springs to allow tuning the forks to every condition possible. Even the factory teams don't have this much tuning variation available to them with their forks.

Fox Factory swingarm and 17.75 inch negative spring AirShoxs on Larry Wosick's CR 250R Honda.

The forks are available in standard length with 12 inches of travel. Optional dampening rods are also available for 11 inches or 13 inches of travel, allowing anyone to match their present rear travel or build a bike which has more travel than the latest factory bikes. Jim Turner has been racing his bike with 13 inches of travel at each end, but it must be remembered that for this much travel to be manageable in tight turns and on slow tracks the suspension must be tuned in initial travel for a somewhat soft static setting so ride height will be in the 10-11 inch range and the bike will be much easier to control. Despite this decrease in ride height to levels more equal to those of shorter travel suspension, the longer travel suspension will still retain the ability to track better across rough ground, since it has more travel available to follow the contours of the ground, giving the rider more control and traction. For high-speed tracks the ride height of the suspension can and should be increased to compensate for the faster speeds and resulting harder impact with large bumps.

The Fox Factory Forks are avilable For Honda CRs and Yamaha YZs at a price of $439.00 complete. For the serious professional rider they are well worth the price for a piece of equipment which will put him on equal terms with what the best factory riders are using.

Moto-X Fox has always been acknowledged as the leader in rear suspension technology, particularly with Fox AirShox which has become the standard of the pro motocross ranks. The 17.5 inch AirShox (99-1750) will bolt right on to the production CR Honda swingarm and has been used by nearly all the factory Team Honda riders from Lackey to Smith and Tripes on their works bikes and production bikes since 1977.

Now available is a new negative spring 17.75 inch AirShox (99-1775) which provides a little different spring rate for riders who can tell the difference. It costs Fox more to manufacturer this shock though, but it sells for the same price as the other model AirShoxs.

Pictured here on Jim's bike are the all-new Fox Factory Shocks. Working on the deCarbon principle with external coil springs, the Fox Factory Shocks should set new standards in their field for performance, tunability, reliability and ease of maintenance. Dampening is adjustable for both compression

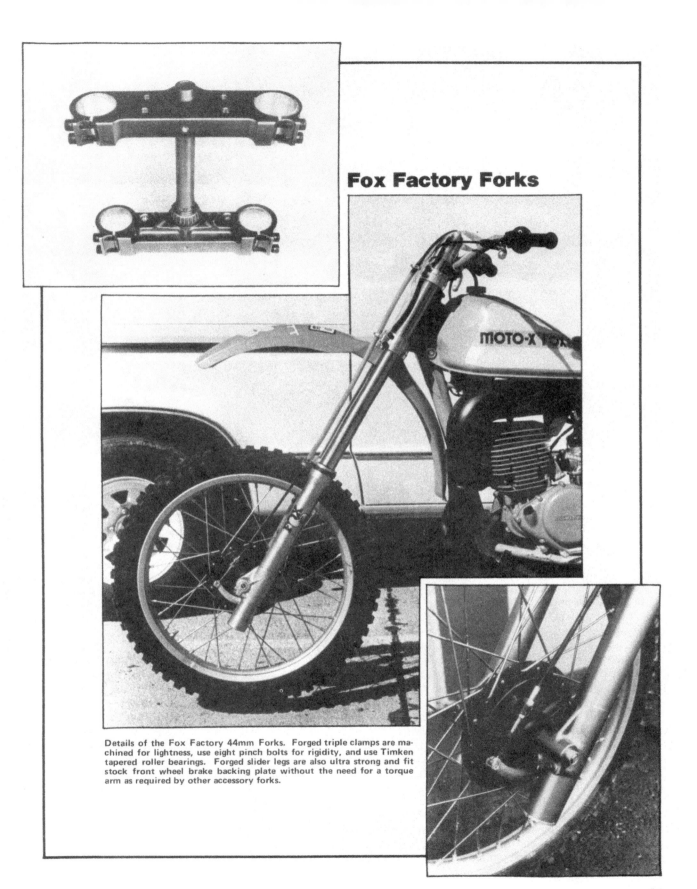

Fox Factory Forks

Details of the Fox Factory 44mm Forks. Forged triple clamps are machined for lightness, use eight pinch bolts for rigidity, and use Timken tapered roller bearings. Forged slider legs are also ultra strong and fit stock front wheel brake backing plate without the need for a torque arm as required by other accessory forks.

Marty Smith's 360cc Mugen kitted 1979 National bike.

and rebound, while various rate two-stage coil springs are available, including straight rate or progressive rate main springs. The Fox Factory Shocks will be available with a choice of either remote mounting resevoirs or piggyback resevoirs attached to the shock body. The Fox Factory Shocks are being offered as an alternative to the AirShox in order to provide the pro-caliber rider a suspension unit which only needs to be dialed-in once and then left alone The price of the Fox Factory Shocks is less than a pair of AirShoxs.

The final suspension component on Jim's Honda is the new Fox Factory Swingarm which is designed to work with 17.75 inch shocks. Once again, here is a component which has been designed to be better than anything else presently available, even on the factory bikes when it comes to comparing strength, performance and light weight. The swingarm is built up of welded aircraft quality 6061 extruded aluminum alloy, heat-treated to T-6 to offer the strongest and most rigid swingarm assembly possible. Wheelbase is increased for more stable handling and better straight line tracking ability, while rear wheel travel is 13 inches.

That just about covers everything as far as what is required to upgrade the stock suspension on a CR 250R Honda to a caliber which is even better than the latest factory bikes.

There are other parts on the bike which are changed and any serious pro-caliber rider should consider making these improvements to his bike to improve performance and reliability. These include the use of ultra-strong Sun rims and heavy-duty spokes, and the replacement of the stock "Saddleback Roadrace Specials" with real motocross tires like those from Metzeler. Also installed is a Gunner Gasser throttle to prevent a snagged throttle cable, and all cables are Terry Cables for smooth operation. All these parts are available from Moto-X Fox.

In the engine department there really isn't much that needs to be done to the stock motor. It already produces more than enough power, though it does come on a little peaky and this is, perhaps, its only real fault. The remedy is to replace the stock Keihin with a 36mm Mikuni carburetor kit from Fox. There is no change in top-end power, but the Mikuni is able to carburate a little better in mid-range than the Keihin carburetor which in turn helps smooth out the powerband.

An additional gain in mid-range power for the CR 250R,R2 comes from the use of a Turner Racing exhaust system. Jim's brother Paul hand builds these beautiful pipes which have been used by many of the major factory teams. The Honda pipe smooths out and broadens mid-range power at a slight sacrafice to top-end power, but the trade off is well worth, it. The Turner Racing pipe is also about a pound lighter than the stock Honda pipe. An additional weight savings of 1 to 2 pounds can be achieved with a Turner Racing aluminum muffler. The pipe sells for $116.95 and the muffler for $35.95. You can order them directly from Turner Racing, 1715 Freedom Boulevard, P.O Box 1119, Freedom, CA 95019, USA.

Now comes the really interesting part. Moto-X Fox has a spare 360cc CR Honda which Jim will be running in International races in Europe as well as the 500cc Nationals. If you remember from rumors, 1979 was the year Honda was supposed to bring out an Open class production bike, but obviously never did. Either Honda felt the marketing potential of an Open class bike wasn't large enough, or a complete new engine design was required because the basic 250cc engine's lower end wasn't strong enough. Both reasons probably applied.

Anyway, to make a long story short, Mr. Honda has a son who is deeply involved in motocross and decided to form his own company to manufacture hop-up kits for Honda dirt bikes. Because they wanted to keep the two companies separate, young Honda's company is named Mugen. In Japan the company Mugen is now marketing a 360cc chrome plated cylinder, piston, rod assembly, primary gears and other parts needed to make the conversion. It is obvious from the design and finish of the kit that it isn't a backyard project, but probably originated from inside the Honda company itself. Why the kit hasn't been incorporated into Honda's production bike lineup can be accounted for by the fact the Mugen kit comes with redesigned gears to increase transmission strength and a letter of caution stressing the need to constantly replace certain other parts which may be at their design stress maximum.

Presently the Mugen engine kits are not available in America and if they were, the price would probably be somewhere in the $800-1200 range. Moto-X Fox might be convinced to import the kit for sale if response for it were large enough.

For the time being though, Moto-X Fox is concerning itself with improving the suspensions of production bikes like the Honda CR 250R, R2. And with the new line of Fox Factory suspension components it is possible for the privateer rider to at last have equipment which is at least equal to, if not whole lot better than what the factory stars have on their exotic works bikes.

Mugen address:

Mugen Co. Ltd.
2-15-11 Hizaore Machi
Asaka Shi Saitama Ken
Japan

Above: A close-up look at the 360cc Mugen reed valve inducted cylinder. The complete kit bolts onto a RC or CR 250 Honda.

FOX ALUMINUM MUFFLER

FOX FACTORY SHOCKS

GUNNER GASSER THROTTLE

TERRY CABLES

MAGURA LEVERS

MOTO-X FOX HANDLEBARS

FOX FACTORY FORKS

DUNLOP TIRES

Tuner Mike McAndrews and rider Larry Wosick with their Moto-X Fox CR 250R National bike utilizing Fox Factory suspension components and Moto-X Fox accessories.

PREPARING THE CR HONDA FOR COMPETITION

FOX F.I.M. SIDE NUMBER PANELS

FOX AIRSHOX

FOX FACTORY SWINGARM

FOX DELUXE GRIPS

SCOTT/PETTY FENDERS

FOX TANK STICKERS

SUN RIMS

METZELER TIRES

POLY-AIR FILTERS

FOX SEAT COVER

GOLDEN SPECTRO OILS

BOSCH SPARK PLUGS

MIKUNI CARBURETOR

ADDITIONAL MODIFICATION AND PREPARATION TIPS FOR THE HONDA CR

You may have noticed on some of the works Hondas and on the Team Moto-X Fox prepared CR-250Rs the installation of an upper chain roller mounted to the frame, similar to the lower chain roller which comes standard on the CR-125R and CR-250R bikes. Team Honda mechanic Bill Buchka first employed this on Brad Lackey's RC-450-78 works bike to guard against possible chain derailment problems which could be brought about by the RC-450's somewhat spindley lightweight aluminum swingarm. The need for the upper chain roller to control chain slop caused by centrifical force before the chain is fed onto the countershaft sprocket is probably more critical than the need for the lower roller. There is the chain roller inside the swingarm chain guard which helps to feed the chain onto the rear drive sprocket.

This new upper chain roller is needed on a CR equipped with the stock Honda swingarm, particularly if you have already been experiencing thrown chain problems, more than likely caused by swingarm flex. A stronger swingarm like the Fox Factory Swingarm

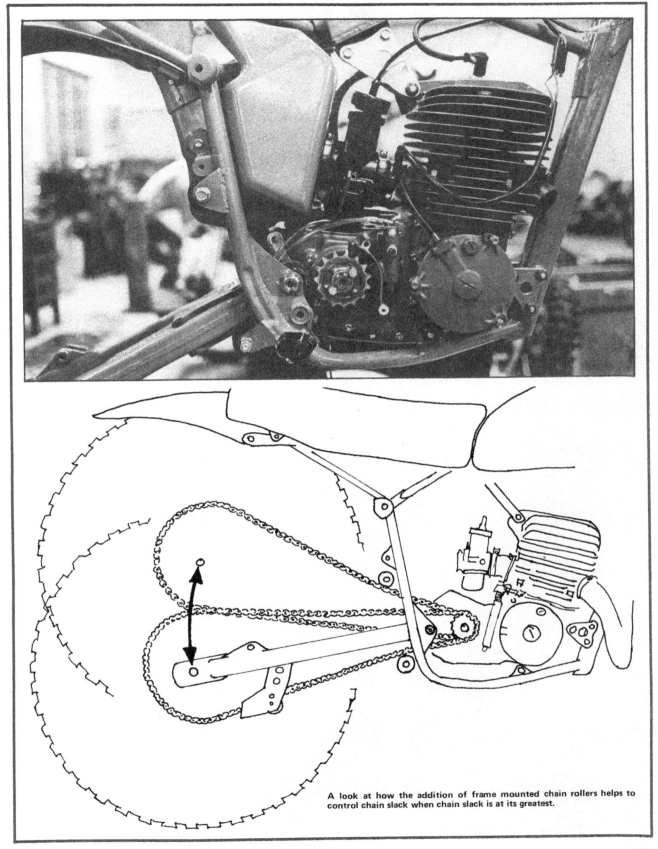

A look at how the addition of frame mounted chain rollers helps to control chain slack when chain slack is at its greatest.

will cure the problem of stock swingarm flex and the resulting problem of thrown chains. You'll also be reducing the weight of your bike and improving its handling in the process. For the added insurance the upper chain roller offers, Team Moto-X Fox continues to use them on their own bikes in addition to the use of a Fox Factory Swingarm and chain problems are non-existant.

You can fashion your own upper chain roller bracket out of a couple pieces of sheet steel and tube as pictured. Moto-X Fox can supply you with the roller bearing skateboard wheel which is part no. 01-1000. A replacement nylon roller to use instead of the stock aluminum lower is available under part no. 01-1006.

Team Moto-X Fox tuner Mike McAndrews uses aluminum plate to fabricate stronger chain guides and upper engine braces which are triangulated for increased rigidity. An aluminum ring is also used outside the plastic airbox to reinforce the air filter mount. Templates are pictured.

Special heavy-duty clutch springs are now available from Moto-X Fox to solve clutch slipping problems on both the CR-125R and CR-250R models under part no. 70-4006.

Here are details of the chain roller guides which were first used on Brad Lackey's RC 450-78 and are now used by Team Moto-X Fox on their CR 125R and CR 250R bikes.

Two plates need to be made for the chain guide, one for each side. Aluminum tubing or drilled bar stock is used to space the plates apart, and either stock Honda aluminum rollers or Moto-X Fox skateboard rollers can be used at the bottom of the chain guide for chain drag. Mike McAndrews cuts up old number plates the same shape as the template and lines the inside of the chain guide assembly to reduce noise and wear.

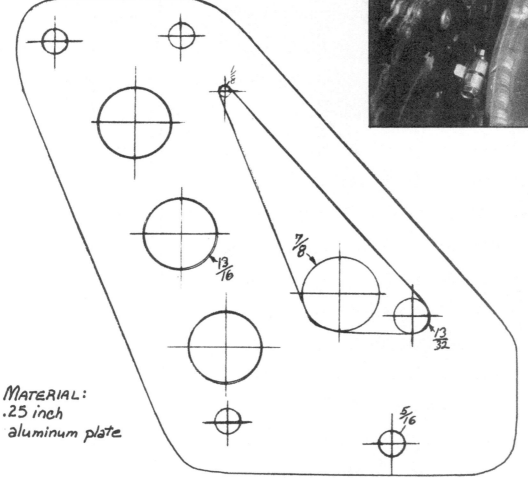

$\frac{13}{16}$

$\frac{7}{8}$

$\frac{13}{32}$

$\frac{5}{16}$

MATERIAL:
.25 inch
aluminum plate

HONDA CR 250 R CHAIN GUIDE

SCALE	DATE	VENDOR	APPROVED BY	DRAWN BY
1:1	5-1-79	N.A.	MOTO-X FOX	MIKE McANDREWS

FACTORY INC.

Fox Factory Incorporated proprietary rights are included in the information disclosed herein. Recipient by accepting this document agrees that neither this document nor the information disclosed herein nor any part thereof shall be reproduced or transferred to other documents or used or disclosed to others for manufacturing or for any other purpose except as specifically authorized by Fox Factory Inc.

FOX FACTORY, INC. 520 McGLINCY LANE CAMPBELL, CA 95008 PHONE (408) 371-1221	REVISION	DRAWING NUMBER

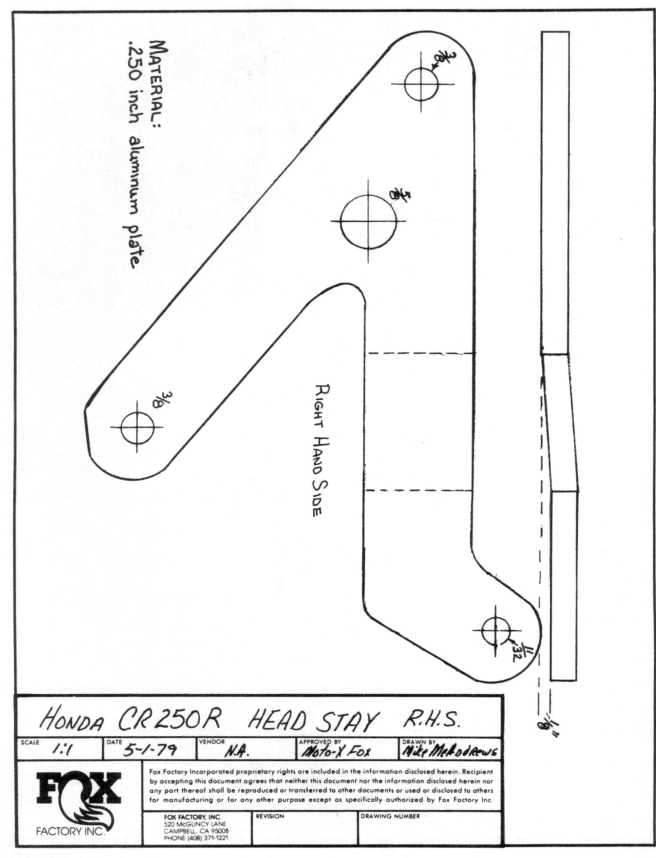

MATERIAL:
.250 inch aluminum plate

RIGHT HAND SIDE

3/8

1/8"

HONDA CR250R HEAD STAY R.H.S.

SCALE 1:1	DATE 5-1-79	VENDOR N.A.	APPROVED BY Moto-X Fox	DRAWN BY Mike McAndrews

FOX FACTORY INC.

FOX FACTORY, INC.
520 McGLINCY LANE
CAMPBELL, CA 95008
PHONE (408) 371-1221

REVISION	DRAWING NUMBER

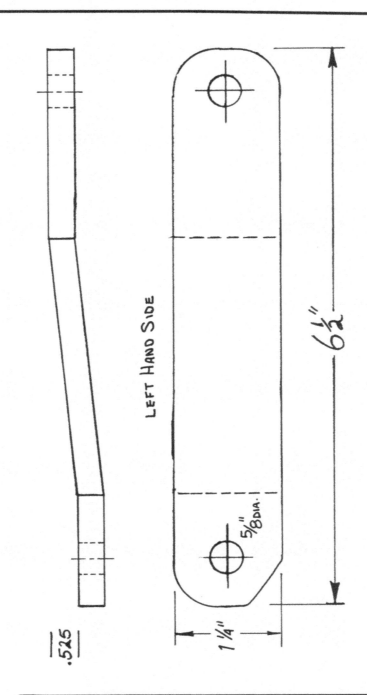

MATERIAL : .250 INCH ALUMINUM PLATE

LEFT HAND SIDE

.525

6½"

5/8" DIA.

1¼"

NOTE: DON'T MARK OR DRILL HOLE BEFORE BENDING METAL.

HONDA CR 250 R HEAD STAY L.H.S.				
SCALE 1:1	DATE 5-1-79	VENDOR N.A.	APPROVED BY MOTO-X FOX	DRAWN BY Mike McAndrews

FOX FACTORY INC.

FOX FACTORY, INC.
520 McGLINCY LANE
CAMPBELL, CA 95008
PHONE (408) 371-1221

REVISION

DRAWING NUMBER

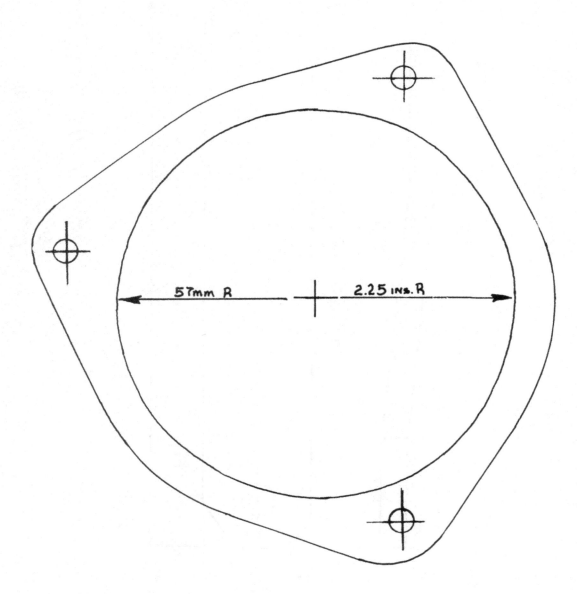

57mm R | 2.25 ins. R

MATERIAL: .125 inch aluminum plate

HONDA CR 250 R AIRBOX RING

SCALE 1:1	DATE 5-1-79	VENDOR N.A.	APPROVED BY Moto-X Fox	DRAWN BY Paul Turner

FACTORY INC.

FOX FACTORY, INC.
520 McGLINCY LANE
CAMPBELL, CA 95008
PHONE (408) 371-1221

REVISION	DRAWING NUMBER

You can build a smoother operating floating rear brake torque arm similar to the works RC Hondas and the Moto-X Fox team bikes by employing aluminum or steel tubing with threaded spherical rod end bearings at each end. This will also allow you to adjust the lenght of the torque arm to match the distance from swingarm pivot to rear wheel axle for ideal full-floating rear brake geometry. You will be able to find the parts you need at a large commercial bearing house, or from Precision Bearing, 2901 Cedar Avenue, Long Beach, CA 90806, phone (213) 427-2375, catalogue $2.00.

Above: Moto-X Fox fabricates its own rear brake torque arm for smoother operation and to equal the distance from swingarm pivot point to rear wheel axle. Below left: Moto-X Fox gas pressure guages offer completely accurate adjustment of suspension pressures. Below: Steel rod is used to fabricate a guard to prevent rider's boot from catching on brake actuator rod.

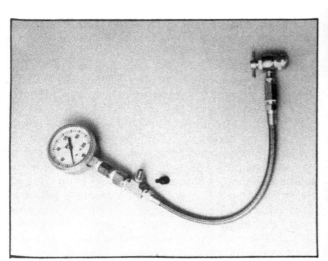

DUNLOP SPORTS K88HT   DUNLOP SPORTS K88   DUNLOP SPORTS SENIOR   DUNLOP K-190 SPORTS

The 1979 model CR-250R2 engine comes with a grooved cylinder exhaust port manifold to help keep dirt from being sucked through the joint and into the cylinder by reverse pressure waves in the exhaust tract. Some dirt can still get in and sealing the header pipe to the exhaust manifold with silicon sealer will make certain that dirt won't be sucked in, causing excessive wear to the engine.

Six different ignition systems are availbable to fit the CR-250R beginning with three labeled A,B, and C during the 1978 season and C,E, and F in 1979. By matching a similarly lettered lower ignition unit on the engine (letter is stamped on the timing cover) with the same letter on the frame mounted black box you can be sure that timing advance specifications for the ignition system will be within factory tolerances. Mis-matching a lower ignition unit of one letter with the black box of another letter will alter the timing and advance curve of the engine's ignition system. This allows Honda to change advance curves for various prototype engine designs they are testing, but offers no advantage on the production CR-250R where the best advance curve requires the letters correspond on the upper and lower ignition units.

The ignition systems on 1978 CR-250R and 1979 CR-250R2 bikes prior to no. 0853 were designed to cut out at high RPMs to prevent over-reving. This causes an audible popping sound when the engine was hot. Though performance wasn't being affected, not too many people liked that popping going on since it sounded like something was wrong in the ignition system. After bike no. 0853, the ignition was redesigned and the over-rev ignition cut off feature changed so that the ignition retarded itself instead at high RPMs to prevent over-reving. Neither system offers a power advantage over the other.

When Team Honda races with a production CR-250R engine they seem to favor the "E" model ignition system since they feel it might have a slight torque advantage over the other ignitions available.

Most Team Riders prefer the 1978 CR-250R cylinder because of its slight top-end horsepower advantage. The 1979 CR-250R2 cylinder produces more torque and mid-range power because of its slightly flatter exhaust port shape and a bridged intake port. With either cylinder the R2's new etched reed valve assembly offers more response and is the one to use.

The purpose of this book is to provide you with information regarding special modifications and procedures needed to keep your Honda CR-125R or CR-250R up to date in the highly competitve world and amid the constantly changing technical advancements of professional motocross. For detailed information regarding the general maintenance and rebuilding of the CR Hondas you should get a copy of the excellent official Honda shop manuals available from your local Honda dealer. Together with this book, the Honda shop manuals will provide you with all the information you need to build and maintain a reliable and competive motocross bike.

Jimmy Ellis on his Fox AirShox equipped Honda. Below: The new Fox Factory Shocks.

TUNING THE SUSPENSION

The most important part of a dirt bike, even more important than the power of the engine, is the bike's suspension. This is the one system on the motorcycle which is in constant use, governing the handling of the bike and just how fast you can go across rough terrain. A dirt bike's suspension needs to perform faultlessly and offer enough tunability that it can be adjusted to the desires of the rider and the conditions of the race track.

Unfortunately, the stock CR Honda suspension is the only major compromise on an otherwise excellent and highly competitive motorcycle. The st-

ock suspension components hardly do much more than attach the wheels to the frame and provide for virtually no adjustment whatsoever. We won't even discuss the stock XR Honda's suspension and trying to improve it, because as the chapter on the XR bikes points out, if you are serious about racing this bike you'll have to go all out for a new frame and better performing long travel-suspension components.

The first place to begin in making improvements to a production CR is with the installation of air fork caps. These are available from Moto-X Fox under part number 39-1025 for both the CR-125R

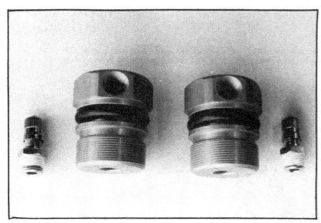

Moto-X Fox Honda gas fork caps.

and CR-250R. The installation of air caps will offer you some adjustability of the stock Showa forks for both ride height and spring rate, particularly since the stock springs sag out very quickly in use.

Air caps are an inexpensive way to improve your front forks, but if your riding skill warrants it you'll want to replace the stock Showa forks with a better fork assembly like the completely adjustable air/ spring Fox Factory Forks. Besides increased performance, Fox Factory Forks can provide you with additional travel at 12 or 13 inches and are extremely strong and flex free.

The rear suspension of the CR Hondas need help too. The first place to begin is replace the stock Showa gas charged shock which is only slightly adjustable for preload, for a shock absorber assembly which is completely adjustable for ride height, spring rate and dampening. The Fox AirShox is the one shock assembly used by the majority of Team Honda riders on their bikes. The new Fox Factory Shock is a coil-over design deCarbon reservoir shock with the same adjustability features as the AirShox, but for the rider who only wants to dial his rear suspension in once and then leave it alone.

To improve the handling of your CR even further you'll want to install a Fox Factory Swingarm. Besides reducing weight over the stock steel swingarm and offering improved strength for better handling and less chain problems caused by flex, the Fox factory Swingarm can give you either 12 or 13 inches of rear wheel travel depending upon selected shock length.

The most important goals to aim for when setting up your Honda's suspension for riding are the proper ride height and spring rate. Ride height is crucial, particularly with long travel suspension, since if the sits up too high it will be difficult to ride and corner properly. A bike with too much ride height will also handle poorly since weight transfer between wheels under braking and accelerating will be intensified, causing drastic changes in wheelbase, fork rake and steering angle.

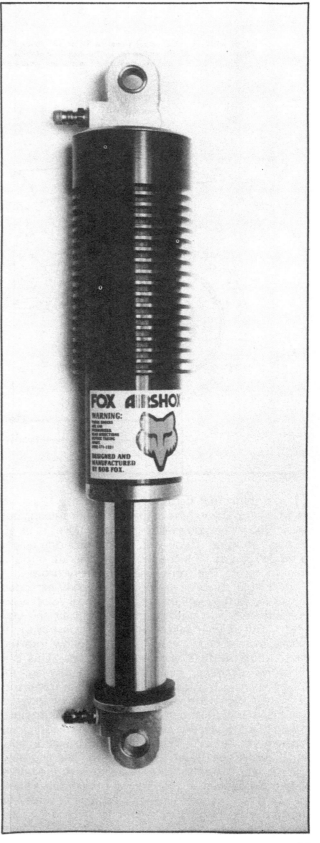

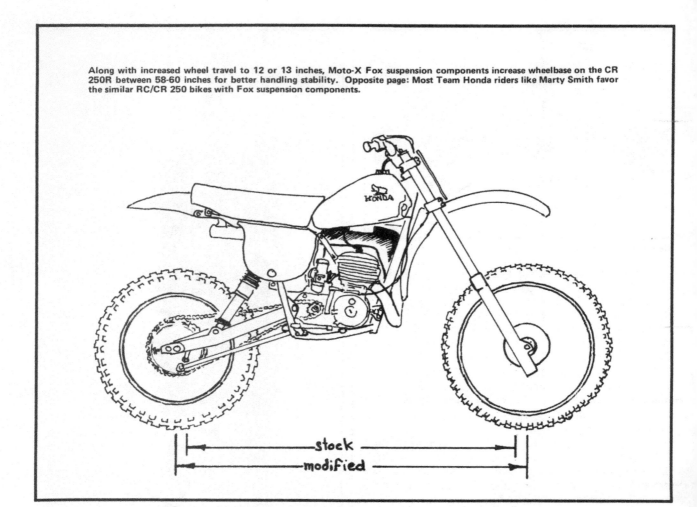

Along with increased wheel travel to 12 or 13 inches, Moto-X Fox suspension components increase wheelbase on the CR 250R between 58-60 inches for better handling stability. Opposite page: Most Team Honda riders like Marty Smith favor the similar RC/CR 250 bikes with Fox suspension components.

stock
modified

Don't think that because your bike has 12 inches of wheel travel you have all of that travel sticking out under you when you're riding for the travel to be effective. Imagine if you will, your bike's ride height is topped out at 12 inches as you accelerate out of a smooth turn. The front wheel suddenly drops into a small hole. Since your forks are already extended out as far as they will go, the front wheel could wash out sideways with nothing under it but air and you crash. But if your bike's ride height is set as say 9 inches, instead of 12, your forks can follow into the contour of the hole and retain traction. This is a simplified example, because other factors are involved as well, but it is a fact that a long travel suspensioned bike with a couple of inches of lowered ride height will track better across rough ground since it won't be topping out as often to loose traction.

Where you set your ride height at depends on how much suspension travel you have available and how tall you are. It only makes sense to have the bike's height low enough so that you can touch the ground for starts and maintaining your balance in turns. A standard ride height setting though, for a 12-inch travel bike, might be 2-3 inches from top out at each

end with your weight centered on the footpegs.

Setting the ride height at the front forks depends upon the design of the forks being used. If the forks are only suspended by internal coil springs, then the ride height is adjusted by altering the length of the springs. Springs can be cut to lower the ride height, or short pieces of springs or spacers can be added on top of the springs to increase the ride height. Fork springs can fatigue with use and decrease in lengtht, causing a corresponding drop in ride height. The stock Honda Showa for springs have a habit of fatiguing. Good fork springs like those in Fox Factory Forks do not.

An easy way to adjust ride height if your fork springs sink down too far is to install a set of air fork caps, which is common practice for the stock Showa forks. By lightly filling the forks with 5-10 PSI of air or gas the proper ride height can be dialed in. Spring rate will be affected somewhat though, depending on air pressure and oil volume.

A true air/spring front fork suspension offers the rider the most variables for fine tuning the suspension. This is because the internal steel springs are designed to be a lighter weight to work in conjunction

with air pressure and provide the most desirable progressive spring rate curve. Ride height is usually adjusted with 18-22 PSI of air in the forks when the forks are fully extended (bike on center stand and front wheel off ground, so internal volume of forks is constant). The fork springs come into work as soon as the forks are compressed, but the springs are soft enough that most of the tuning can be done with the air pressure and oil volume in the forks.

Setting the ride height on the rear suspension is accomplished by moving the spring preload adjuster collar on coil-over spring shocks either up or down to gain the required ride height. The stock Showa shocks do offer you a slight range of preload adjustment, but a far greater preload range is available with better quality shocks like the Fox Factory Shocks.

You should realize that a change in spring free lenght (uncompressed) and a change to a softer or firmer spring of the same length will alter ride height, as well as affect the spring rate throughout the entire suspension travel. So when you change spring rate you can expect to have to re-adjust the ride height.

Just changing the preload setting to alter ride height

does not affect spring rate (also termed spring weight) If you are using progressive rate springs though, a large adjustment in spring preload can alter the point in suspension travel at which spring rates change.

Check that too much spring preload (the shortening of the installed length of the spring beyond what the spring and shock were designed for) does not lead to complete coil bind of the entire spring as the shock nears bottoming out. This will drive your spring rate to infinity and most likely result in broken springs. The shock should bottom out on its bump rubber before the spring coil binds. The only way to check this is to put the shock assembly in a press, taking precautions that the shock won't slip out while it is being compressed.

Progressive rate springs do work on the principle of coil binding. With dual springs, the lighter spring will coil bind, transfering the load over to the heavier spring. With a progressively wound spring, the more tightly wound end of the spring will coil bind causing an increase in spring rate in the portion of spring still working. The entire spring assembly should never coil bind completely though to prevent breakage. Even without complete coil bind, progressive

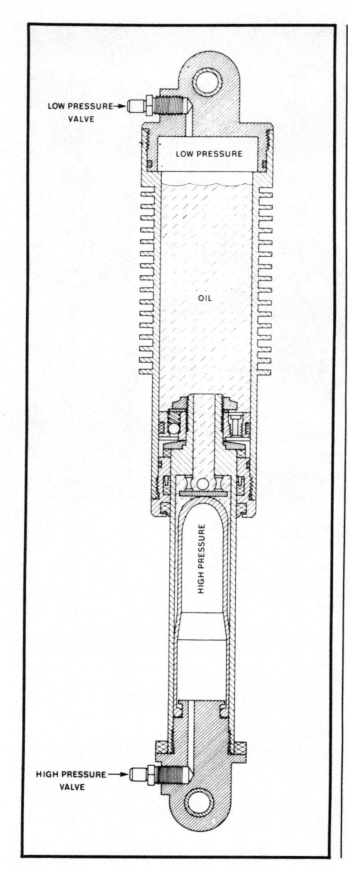

LOW PRESSURE VALVE

LOW PRESSURE

OIL

HIGH PRESSURE

HIGH PRESSURE VALVE

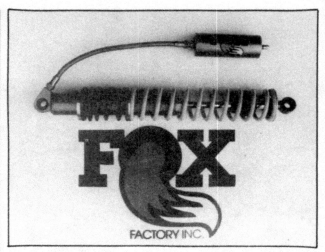

An inside look at the popular Fox AirShox. The dual-stage air spring system offers the most ideal progressive spring rate. Always be sure to charge the high pressure valve first when pressurizing AirShoxs. Above: The new Fox Factory spring shocks. Opposite page: The Fox Factory Swingarm is stronger and lighter than stock to offer improved handling on Hondas, as well as increased rear wheel travel if needed depending on choice of shock length.

rate spring systems are somewhat prone to breakage if the springs are not of good enough quality, and the breakage invariably occurs in the section of spring which coil binds first.

Adjusting ride Height with Fox AirShoxs is extremely simple. It's just a matter of finding the right air pressure setting on the low pressure valve of the Air-Shoxs while the rider is sitting on the bike.

Once ride height has been established for the bike's suspension, the next adjustment is for spring rate. This is done by riding the bike, and better riders adjust the spring rate for every track. The idea is to have the spring rate soft enough so the bike will use all its travel, but not so soft that the suspension bottoms out severely. The bike's suspension should just bottom out on one or two of the worst sections or jumps on the track.

If your bike uses spring forks or shocks, then you may need to carry a selection of different rate or different progression springs to change your suspension for different tracks, or at least try to find a happy medium for the majority of tracks or conditions you'll be racing under.

Fox Factory Forks are the only forks available which offer you the choice of different rate springs for the perfect dialing in of your forks to suit you, your bike and riding conditions. In most instances though, the stock springs which come in Fox Factory Forks will prove to be ideal and won't need to be changed since Moto-X Fox has done a year of testing with Hondas to get the spring rates right.

Fox Factory Shocks come standard with two-stage single rate or progressive rate springs. Most Honda applications will be a bolt-on proposition in regards to the right spring rates, but should you need different rates and progressions of the long and short springs they are available from Moto-X Fox.

The silasto rubber cushion on the dampening shaft of Fox Factory Shocks is an integral part of the spring system of the shock assembly, rather than only being there to protect the internal parts of the shock from possible damage during bottoming out as is the case with other shock designs which employ a short thick rubber bumper. The silasto rubber cushion provides a very smooth transition working as rising rate progressive spring to prevent bottoming of the suspension. The advantage is that a softer rate main spring can then be employed for improved handling response on medium size bumps without fear the main spring will be too soft for large bumps or jumps.

The initial purchase price of Fox Factory Shocks is less than a pair of Fox AirShox. But if you are an experienced rider who plans to re-adjust his suspension each week to suit particular race conditions, then AirShoxs might be a better choice for you. There would be no need to invest in a large selection of different rate coil springs, and the adjustment of air spring rates on the AirShox is a quick and easy job. For riders who compete on the same track conditions each weekend or tend toward a maintenance-free bike they don't have to constantly be adjusting, Fox Factory Shocks might be a better choice.

The Fox Factory Forks are the only forks presently available which offer (3) three optional positive springs and (3) three optional negative springs for perfect dialing-in of the air/spring rate. These forks are also the only forks available on the market with a rebound relief valve similar to those found on some of the factory works bikes forks for better dampening control.

The ease of adjustment for spring rates are what air/spring forks are all about. Air/spring front forks have a progressive spring action which gets stiffer as the forks come close to bottoming out, but they are also soft when extended to react easily to small bumps. By changing the oil volume in the forks you alter the progressive rate of the springs, allowing you to tune for an increased amount of either soft or firm air/spring progression depending on how rough the track is. But you will still retain some small bump or large bump control no matter what type of course you set the forks up for.

Fox AirShoxs make the tuning of the rear suspension even easier. While the low pressure valve helps to adjust ride height and spring rate over smaller bumps, the high pressure setting and oil volume allows the shocks to be adjusted for large bumps and the type of spring rate progression curve desired. The soft pressure setting works independently of the hard pressure setting so the shocks will always have a smooth reaction to small bumps no matter how stiff the hard pressure setting is made. Each setting, hard and soft, remains progressive though, and they over-

Table 1. Fox Airshox Pressure Recommendations (psi)

A. BIKE WEIGHT 170—190 LBS.

RIDER WEIGHT*	SUSPENSION LEVER RATIO							
	1.6	1.7	1.8	1.9	2.0	2.1	2.2	2.3
120 lbs.	53/85	56/90	59/94	62/99	66/106	69/110	72/115	75/120
130 lbs.	55/88	58/93	61/98	65/104	69/110	72/115	75/120	78/125
140 lbs.	57/91	60/96	64/102	68/109	72/115	75/120	78/125	82/131
150 lbs.	59/94	62/99	66/106	70/112	74/118	78/125	81/130	85/136
160 lbs.	62/99	65/104	69/110	73/117	77/123	81/130	85/136	89/142
170 lbs.	64/102	67/107	72/115	76/122	80/128	84/134	88/141	92/147
180 lbs.	66/106	70/112	75/120	79/126	83/133	87/139	91/146	95/152
190 lbs.	68/109	72/115	77/123	81/130	85/136	89/142	94/150	98/157
200 lbs.	71/114	75/120	80/128	84/134	88/141	92/147	97/155	101/162
210 lbs.	73/117	77/123	82/131	86/138	91/146	95/152	100/160	104/166
220 lbs.	75/120	79/126	84/134	90/142	94/150	98/157	103/165	107/171

B. BIKE WEIGHT 190—210 LBS.

RIDER WEIGHT*	SUSPENSION LEVER RATIO							
	1.6	1.7	1.8	1.9	2.0	2.1	2.2	2.3
120 lbs.	56/90	60/96	63/101	66/106	70/112	73/117	76/122	80/128
130 lbs.	58/92	62/99	65/104	69/110	72/115	76/122	79/126	83/133
140 lbs.	60/96	64/102	68/109	72/115	75/120	79/126	83/133	87/139
150 lbs.	62/99	66/106	70/112	74/118	78/125	82/131	86/138	90/144
160 lbs.	65/104	69/110	73/117	77/123	81/130	85/136	89/142	93/149
170 lbs.	67/107	71/114	75/120	79/126	83/133	87/139	92/147	96/154
180 lbs.	69/110	73/117	77/123	82/131	86/138	90/144	95/152	100/160
190 lbs.	71/114	75/120	79/126	84/134	88/141	93/149	98/157	103/165
200 lbs.	74/118	78/125	82/131	87/139	91/146	96/154	101/162	106/170
210 lbs.	76/122	80/128	85/136	90/144	95/152	99/158	104/166	109/174
220 lbs.	78/125	85/133	88/141	93/149	98/157	102/163	107/171	112/179

C. BIKE WEIGHT 210—230 LBS.

RIDER WEIGHT*	SUSPENSION LEVER RATIO							
	1.6	1.7	1.8	1.9	2.0	2.1	2.2	2.3
120 lbs.	58/93	62/99	66/106	70/112	73/117	76/122	80/128	83/133
130 lbs.	60/96	64/102	68/109	72/115	76/122	80/128	83/133	87/139
140 lbs.	63/101	67/107	71/114	75/120	79/126	83/133	87/139	91/146
150 lbs.	65/104	69/110	73/117	77/123	81/130	85/136	90/144	94/150
160 lbs.	68/109	72/115	76/122	80/128	84/134	88/141	93/149	98/157
170 lbs.	70/112	74/118	78/125	82/131	87/139	92/147	97/155	101/162
180 lbs.	72/115	76/122	81/130	85/136	90/144	94/150	99/158	104/166
190 lbs.	74/118	78/125	83/133	88/141	93/149	97/155	102/163	106/170
200 lbs.	76/122	81/130	86/138	91/146	96/154	100/160	105/168	109/174
210 lbs.	78/125	83/133	88/141	93/149	98/157	103/165	108/173	112/179
220 lbs.	81/130	86/138	91/146	96/154	101/162	106/170	111/178	116/186

* Add approximately 10 lbs. for weight of riding equipment.

** Latest tip for *pros* and *fast experts only*: set *high* pressure about 10% higher than shown in Table above. *No change* to *low* pressure.

lap smoothly. Now you can begin to understand why the Fox AirShox is such a good shock and the favorite of so many top riders.

Both the Fox Factory Shock and the Fox AirShox offer progressive and adjustable dampening in both compression and rebound. In most cases you will not need to change dampening from what will come standard in the shock.

For most riders, attempting to adjust a shock's dampening is extremely difficult since so many factors are involved...among them is the spring rate, impact force, shaft speed, rider's weight and so on. And then dampening usually is made softer in compression than rebound, since the shock needs to react more quickly in the compression mode to absorb in the spring the force of the bump. Usually you want only a little compression dampening to allow the springs to do their job, but enough rebound dampening to prevent the back end of the bike from kicking. Progressive rate springs make the whole job of dialing-in dampening even more complicated to the point that a huge computer program would be needed to gather all the facts and variables and still be able to make a ball park guess. The human brain of an experienced rider can do this guessing a lot easier in a lot less time with test riding. Moto-X Fox has already done all the necessary testing and the stock dampening supplied with each shock is pretty close to perfect.

When making dampening changes, always use the lightest weight (usually no. 5 or no. 10 weight) suspension fluid possible. This will help to reduce foaming and prevent lowering in fluid viscosity from heat which can lead to dampening fade.

It is important to keep accurate measurement of both the oil volumes and air pressures you are running in your suspension components. A change in oil volume of just 1cc or change in air pressure of just 1 PSI can be felt in the preformance of the related suspension components. For this purpose a chemist's flask for measuring oil precisely and a Fox pressure guage for adjusting air is very important.

The use of Nitrogen gas is desired in suspension components over the use of air. Regular air contains moisture which can be corrosive to internal metal parts, and the Oxygen in air can cause seals to deteriorate more quickly. Air can also affect some types of fork oils. Nitrogen has the desirable properties of being a constant inhert gas. In a pinch though, compressed air is OK, particularly since good riders maintain a regular maintenance schedule on their bikes when it comes to the replacement of seals and oils.

Table 2. Suspension Lever Ratios for Certain Bikes (Stock)

BIKE	SUSPENSION LEVER RATIO
Honda CR-250R	1.8
Husky GP ('77)	1.8
KTM ('76, '77)	2.2
Maico AW ('76, '77)	2.2
Suzuki RM-B & RM-C	1.9

$$SLR = \frac{\text{rear wheel travel}}{\text{shock shaft travel}}$$

Example:

Honda CR250-R
  Rear wheel travel = 11"
  Shock shaft travel = 6"

$$SLR = \frac{11}{6} = 1.8$$

NOTE: This Table for general reference only. Your bike may have mid-year factory modifications or other model changes. Double-check your particular bike's SLR as shown. *These SLR's do not apply with 17½ shocks (except the Honda CR-250R which has 17½" shocks standard).*

CARBURETION

You Can't Expect To Win
If Your Bike Isn't Running Right.

The production CR Hondas come equipped with Kehin carburetors, a 32mm in the case of the CR 125R and a 36mm on the CR-250R. These do a fairly good job of mixing the fuel. Kehin carburetors are also used on the RC factory works bikes. We have found though, that the replacement of the stock Kehin carburetor with a Mikuni will provide for a little better mid-range throttle response and power. At full throttle there is no measurable difference between a Kehin and a Mikuni.

Moto-X Fox does offer a replacement bolt-on 36 mm Mikuni for the CR-250R Honda under part number 36-0005. We have also found that the CR-125R Honda is under carbureted with its stock 32mm Kehin and will perform noticibly better with a 34mm Mikuni which is available under part number 34-0003.

Both the Japanese Kehin and the Japanese Mikuni are very similar in design and the rules for tuning and jetting them are the same. Parts like main jets, needles and needle jets are particular to each manufacturer and are not interchangable, nor are parts like jets labeled alike. Jetting parts for Kehin carburetors are available from your local Honda dealer and jetting parts for Mikuni carburetors are available from Yamaha, Suzuki and Kawasaki dealers. A new throttle cable, available from Moto-X Fox, will be needed if your are replacing a Kehin carburetor with a Mikuni.

Before attempting to jet your engine, be sure the float level in the carburetor is properly adjusted. if it isn't jetting the engine properly will be hampered. Also, the float bowl breather/overflow pipe needs to be clear of obstructions and the air filter must be clean. The spark plug must also be new and of the proper heat range for your engine (Champion N-2G or NGK B9EV or Bosch W3CS).

Consult the diagram to see in what range of throttle operation the main jet, jet needle and pilot circuit operate. The pilot circuit should be set first to assure lubrication to the engine, then the main jet followed by the jet needle and if needed, the needle jet. For

	THROTTLE			
	1/4	1/2	3/4	Full
Main jet				
Jet needle				
Pilot air screw				

CARBURETOR
(1) Rubber cap
(2) Top set
(3) Throttle valve set
(4) Jet needle set
(5) Starter valve set
(6) Screw set
(7) Air vent tube
(8) Float valve set
(9) Slow jet
(10) Needle jet set
(11) Main jet holder
(12) Main jet
(13) Float set
(14) Float chamber set
(15) Over flow tube

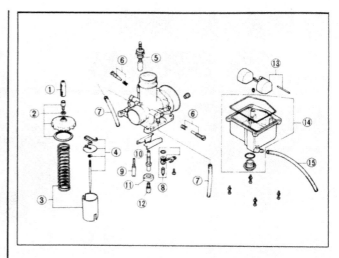

tuning, the bike will be needed to be taken out to a track or road where it can be run at full throttle in the top gears for a good distance (1-2 miles).

PILOT CIRCUIT: The pilot air screw, located outside the carburetor (do not confuse with the idle adjustment screw which raises or lowers the throttle slide), governs the jetting circuit from idle or closed throttle up towards ¼ throttle. Turning the screw out will lean out the air mixture, while turning the screw in will richen it. The normal position for the pilot air screw on both Mikuni and Kehin carburetors is 1½ turns backed out from the fully run-in position. You can set the pilot air screw with the engine running in neutral and turning over at a steady throttle setting of 1,000-2,000 RPM. Adjust the pilot air screw out from the fully run-in position until the mixture becomes too rich and the idle speed begins to fall off, then turn the screw about ¼ turn back in to achieve what should be the proper setting. You can now set the idle adjustment screw to a slow speed which will allow the engine to run smoothly without stalling.

MAIN JET: During running the main jet controls fuel supply from ¾ throttle to full throttle. Run the bike at full throttle under load for a good distance, then shut it off quickly with the kill button. Remove the spark plug and check its color. If the color is black or the surface is wet, then the jetting is too rich and you need to go down to the next smaller size main jet. If the color is grey or white, then the main jet is too lean and you need to go up to the next larger size. A chocolate brown to tan color means the main jet is correct.

Additionally, you should be able to feel or hear if the main jet is correct. If the bike bucks, running erratically with a burbling or popping sound, then it is too rich and you need to go down to the next smaller main jet size which allows it to run smooth and clean. If the main jet is too small the bike will hesitate when given full throttle. It will probably even run faster if you back off the throttle. Consult the spark plug color to confirm that the engine is lean. Keep testing larger size main jets until the engine begins to run rich then go back down one size smaller where the engine runs cleanly to attain the proper main jet size. Don't run an engine in a lean condition too long or serious damage can result. Pre-ignition in the form of a pinging sound from the engine can be an indication of too lean jetting.

JET NEEDLE: The jet needle attached to the throttle slide controls fuel supply between ¼ and ¾ throttle. Once again, run the engine in this throttle range under load on the track for a reasonable distance. Check the spark plug color for the proper chocolate to tan color as described previously. Once again, you should be able to feel and hear if the engine is rich or lean. The needle has five notches and its position in the throttle slide is located by a clip. To make the needle leaner, set the clip in a higher notch which will lower the jet needle further down into the needle jet. Raising the needle will make the engine run richer in mid-range. It is always better to determine the proper jetting by making the engine run rich, then leaning it out just enough so that it runs clean. If the jet needle doesn't provide you with the necessary rich or lean tuning latitude needed in the ¼ to ¾ throttle range, you will probably need to change a larger or smaller needle jet. Also, the jet needles themselves are available in different taper designs to gain even more exacting jetting requirements for particular throttle settings within the jet needle's operating range.

ADDITIONAL CARBURETOR TUNING

Sometimes the carburetor will not allow itself to be jetted properly, or it seems to be jetted properly when held at a constant throttle setting, but not when the throttle is turned on quickly or the engine is accelerating under a load. Assuming the engine is being operated within its intended RPM range the problem could be in the slide cutaway angle which governs how the engine takes or responds to a moving throttle. If the engine feels lean and pings you need to change to a slide with less of a cutaway angle. If the engine feels rich and stumbles you need to change to a slide with more of a cutaway angle. Your dealer will be able to provide you with slides of different cutaway angles.

Changes in slide cutaway can affect the jet needle and needle jet operation since the operation of all three are interrelated. If this happens you will have to work back and forth between the three until the system balances out. Taking the time to get your carburetion perfect is important and worth more than what any trick engine modification might provide.

TRAINING TIPS FROM

MARTY SMITH

Team Honda's Championship Winning Bionic Racer

Any kid who knows anything at all about motocross knows who Marty Smith is. Mention Team Honda and you automatically think of Marty. The two are synonymous. It seems Marty has always ridden for Honda and that's one thing in the sport which will never change. His achievements have helped to make him an inspiration to a whole generation of young American motocrossers.

During the time since joining Team Honda in 1974, Marty has compiled up a record which few riders can ever match, including three U.S. National Championships. He nailed down his first Number one plate in 1974, winning the U.S. 125cc title. He repeated it again in 1975. During the 1976 season Marty competed in selected races of the 125cc World Champion-

ship and though his schedule stateside prevented him from making all the races, he still did well enough to place third overall in the Championship standing. In 1977 Marty nearly pulled off a double title, beating Bob Hannah out for the 500cc National Championship and missing the 250cc crown by a mere handful of points. That 500cc title made Marty the first rider to ever take a National Championship in more than one class. During the 1978 season he came back from a serious Supercross Series accident to take third in the 500cc National Championship.

If you have ever seen Marty in action on the track or in person you'll notice immediately that he is certainly one of the best conditioned riders there are. He never seems to get tired during a race and always maintains a strong, steady pace throughout a day of heated back-to-back 45-minute motos.

There are probably just two favorite methods among the top factory riders for getting into condition to race motocross. Most will try to find an enjoyable compromise between the two. And then some riders will only feel comfortable and not get bored by just doing one thing or another. Your choice may also be governed by the time you have to spend in training or practicing, as well as maintaining a pratice bike.

Many top riders hate to look at a motorcycle during the week, so instead, their training program consists mainly of doing a prescribed set of exercises and running. I think it has been easily proven that running at least half an hour every day will do more for you than any other type of exercising when it comes to getting in condition to motocross.

Marty's method of getting in shape involves riding.

"In past years I never worried about my diet. I never ran. I do like to water ski and play racket ball. But my regular workout for racing was to go out and ride 3-4 days a week. I'd build a track near my house and go and ride on it nearly every day.

"Even today I'll ride as much as 3-4 days a week if I can. I'll change around the course I'm riding on if I get bored with it, or else I'll go somewhere else to another track."

There is no doubt that nothing will get you in better shape for riding than riding, but for many privateers this can be difficult since it usually requires you to have and maintain a separate practice bike. You can practice on your race bike, but it is probably a good idea not to do it more than once a week if you expect it to stay together on Sunday. No doubt, it doesn't need to be mentioned that you should practice on your race bike before you've prepared it for the coming weekend's race, not after preparing it.

"For the Supercross races I have started to do other things besides just riding. I have also started running, because the tracks are so tight and the races are so quick it is easy to get out of breath. Riding a Supercross is like running in a sprint. No matter how good of shape you're in...the pace is so fast...you are bound to get winded. On an outdoor track there is time to catch your breath.

"I still like to play a lot of racket ball. I've started to work out at a gymnasium, too. But ever since I was 11-12 years old I've worked out with wieghts. 10-15 minutes a night. It seemed to help me. I've never gotten tired in a race in my whole life."

I asked Marty about his diet. Were there any hints in what he ate for getting into condition and staying there?

"In past years I never really worried much about my diet, but now that I'm older I realize how important diet can be. I try to stay away from junk foods...things that contain sugar, grease, places like McDonalds and Jack In The Box. I eat lots of wholesome foods now...eggs, steaks, fruits. On race day when I'm thirsty I drink a mixture of Gookinaid E.R.G. and cranberry juice."

And what about vitamins?

"If you do anything sports activated, you need vitamins, whoever you are. Your body can only make so much of its own vitamins and then it runs out. How fast it runs out depends on how active you are. Taking vitamins assures you that your body will have the vitamins it needs, and well as making certain you won't run down on them when you are active.

"When you first start taking them you probably won't notice any difference in how you feel. But after taking them daily every day for a month or so, and then stopping, that's where you can really feel the difference. Vitamins are just good sense insureance for anyone, not just athletes. For anyone that rides motocross, is out on the circuit traveling, or not eating regular balanced meals they have to be necessary!"

So that's the inside scoup on how one of motocross' top athletes gets into shape and stays there. Some of it is fun, some of it takes a little self control, and some of it requires working out hard if you intend to be in as good a shape as the majority of factory riders on the National circuit.

Marty became the first rider in AMA histroy to win National Motocross Championships in more than one class to prove his versatility. Here he is pictured on the special RC 400 which mechanic Dave Arnold built for him for the 1978 Trans-AMA Series.

XR-500

MODIFYING THE HONDA XR FOUR-STROKES

The quest for less air polution, less noise and better fuel economy for dirt bikes in recent years has brought about a resurgent interest in four-stroke engines. The cleaner burning four-stroke engine with its precise valve timing and half the power strokes of a two-stroke engine is certainly a much more economical and cleaner running powerplant. However, for equal displacements the four-stroke engine can not equal the performance of a two-stroke, and even if sanctioning rules allow a four-stroke to run with additional displacement to make up for the horse-power loss the four-stroke engine is still at a disadvantage compared to a two-stroke engine in terms of weight, complexity, and a higher center of gravity. Until the rules of government or sanctioning bodies make it otherwise, two-strokes will remain the do-

minate force in nearly all forms of off-road competition.

Which brings us to the topic of this chapter, that of turning a Honda into a competitive off-road or enduro bike. To my mind the easiest way to put a Honda into the winner's circle is to take a competitive motocrosser like the CR-250R, make the necessary enduro legal modifications to it and go racing. The only difficulty I can see in the whole scheme is the fabrication and installation of a lighting generator on the crankshaft for AMA events. Perhaps the parts from other Honda dirt bike models could be adapted to fit if you have access to a machine shop, but the solution won't be an easy one until someone brings out a simple bolt-on lighting kit for CRs.

Beginning with the 1979 season Honda introduced the new XR line of four-stroke dirt bikes in 185cc, 250cc and 500cc displacements. The pretense of these XR bikes are that they are serious enduro machines. They certainly are among the nicest and most inovative trail bikes going. They might also prove ideal as a beginner's enduro mount. But in their stock underpowered, undersuspensioned and overweight form they can't be considered serious enduro machines for an experienced rider. There is no way a rider of a stock XR can expect to compete with a Dick Burleson, Jack Penton or Frank Gallo on their Husqvarnas or KTMs which are nothing less than full-on motocross bikes with lights and an odometer.

There is not much to be gained in making minor modifications to a stock XR Honda. The reason being the major handicaps the bike imposes on an experienced rider can not be easily corrected with a few simple bolt-on parts like shocks or a swingarm offering slightly longer rear wheel travel. The bike will still be overweight, undersuspended and underpowered. The only solution is in a complete rebuilding of the bike from the frame to the engine. It is a somewhat costly venture which will probably exceed $3000 for the complete bike by the time you're done, but it is the price of building a competive four-stroke Honda.

The place to begin modifying the XR Hondas is with new frame designed for long travel suspension. The Honda Enduro Team has been using C&J precision Products frames on their XRs ever since they got their first pre-production bikes in 1978. The C&J frame kits are available in different forms allowing customer preference to seat height, fork rake, ground clearance, and rear wheel travel ranging from 8.5 to 11.5 inches. They can make it so all the stock XR components like seat and fuel tank bolt right up, but the best kit is probably the one which uses identical CR-250R frame geometry and allows the stock CR components like tank, seat, fenders and forks to bolt right on. The C&J frame kits are 11 pounds lighter than stock.

There is an additional advantage in choosing the C&J frame kit for the XRs which use CR geometry and parts. That is you'll be able to utilize better suspension components like Fox Factory Forks and Fox factory Shocks or Fox AirShox. This is certainly the way to go if you are constructing an XR motocrosser as well and need to get suspension travel up into 11 or 12 inch range. From its stock weight of 271 pounds it would seem reasonable that an XR-500 in lightened motocross form with a C&J frame kit could be gotton down to 230 pounds. Included in C&J's frame kit are aluminum side panels and an inside rear frame splash panel. Other parts like foot pegs, brake pedal and the alloy skid plate are retained from a stock XR.

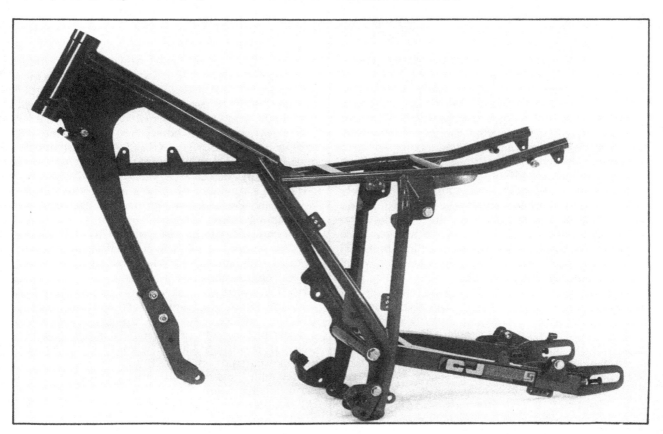

XR-250

Both the XR-250 and XR-500 share the same C&J frame kit, while the XR-185 gets its own frame kit because of its different engine design. Suggested list price for the kit is $645.00.

If you don't already own an XR Honda and plan to build up a new C&J framed bike from the start you should know that your Honda dealer can order you complete engines. It seems Honda has already anticipated a demand for just the XR engines. In this case you should consult your Honda dealer in reguards to the price of an engine compared to a complete bike and go from there. Unless you plan to build an enduro XR using numerous stock components like tank, seats and lights, you probably would be better off just ordering an engine. If you are building an XR motocrosser, then it would certainly be cheaper in the long run to just purchase the engine separate, since the only other stock XR parts you'll need are the left-hand drive rear wheel hub, the foot pegs and rear brake pedal.

Once you've built yourself a good handling XR chassis, and not until then, you can start worrying about putting more horsepower into the XR engine. This turns out to be a very simple operation since it turns out Honda offers High Performance Options, a complete kit of parts to turn the XRs into high performance off-road machines. Parts may be ordered from the kit individually, but it is certainly a better idea to get the complete kit. C&J claims that parts like the High Performance Options exhaust

system from the kit will bolt up easily to their frames.

With the High Performance Options kit, the XR-185 gets a displacement increase from 180cc to 195cc while the 250cc XR is increased to 262cc. This should give the engines adequate power for enduro work in their respective classes, but not for serious motocross. The AMA allows 250cc class four-strokes to run 360cc to be competitive, but Honda isn't taking advantage of this fact which will leave the XR-250 down some five horsepower against the two-strokes in the class. The XR-500 on the other hand, does have enough displacement to be competitive in Open class motocross.

Here is a rundown of what's available in the individual High Performance Options kits available from your Honda dealer:

The complete options package for the XR-185 will raise horsepower to 20.8 @ 9000 RPM, and improvement of 15.6 percent over the stock machine.

Two sub-assemblies are available:

No. I Big Bore Kit. New barrel increases bore from standard 63mm to 65.5mm for total displacement of 194.6cc (180.2cc is stock). The big bore kit includes a bigger piston, with rings and head and base gaskets.

No. II Breathing Kit. The muffler is integral to horsepower gains in the XR-185 and is one pound lighter than the stock unit. Includes heat shield and mounting hardware. AMA enduro noise legal with USDA-approved spark arrestor. Complete replacement airbox increases volume and flow over stock box. High performance unit features three intake holes (standard has two) and cylindrical oiled foam filter element. Also included is new jetting for standard carburetor and optional 56 and 60-tooth rear sprockets and heavy-duty D.I.D. drive chain. (standard sprocket has 58 teeth.)

The XR-250 High Performance Options give you a lot of ways to go -all the way up to 29.8 horsepower @ 9,500 RPM (from stock 24.6 horsepower @ 9,000 RPM) with the complete kit.

Six sub-assemblies are available:

No. I Muffler Kit. Freer flow design and torque chamber offers greatest horsepower gains of any of the other XR-250 sub-assemblies. AMA enduro noise legal, including USDA-approved spark arrestor and mounting hardware.

No. II Big Bore Kit. Includes new cylinder barrel with 76mm bore (2mm over stock) for total displacement of 262cc. Also included: High compression racing piston (raises compression from 9.6:1 to 10.3:1), piston rings, special lightweight wrist pin, special head gasket and base gasket.

No. III Cylinder Head Kit. Ported and matched for increased flow, with 1mm oversize intake valves.

No. IV Carburetor Kit. Large pre-jetted 34mm CR-type racing carb replaces 30.5mm stock unit. Kit includes quick-turn throttle and cable plus carb-mounted direct choke and special carb insulator.

No. V Airbox Kit. New airbox with bigger inlets and bigger air tract to carburetor delivers greater flow capacity. Includes new foam filter element with double the surface area of the stock element.

No. VI Lightweight Crankshaft Kit. Includes lightened and balance crankshaft, cutaway counterbalancers with special tungsten inserts and shaved connecting rod for reduced moment of inertia and 10 to 15 percent increase in engine response.

The High Performance Options Kit for the XR-500 includes enough trick parts to raise horsepower from a stock 35.9 @ 6500 RPM to 40.8 @ 7000 RPM. Individual sub-assemblies are:

No. I Muffler. Specially designed high performance muffler incorporates freer flow design for greatest single horsepower gain of the four XR-500 assemblies High performance muffler is 2.42 pounds lighter than stock, includes USDA-approved spark arrestor and is AMA enduro noise legal.

No. II High Compression Piston Kit. Includes relieved, slipper-type racing piston for compression increase from stock 8.6:1 to 9.5:1. Kit includes piston rings, base gasket and head gasket. Two oversizes available.

No. III Competition Camshaft. Offers increased performance benefits of a longer duration and an additional ten degrees of overlap compared to the stock camshaft.

No. IV Carburetor Kit. Includes larger, prejetted 37mm (stock is 34mm) CR-type competition carburetor with body-mounted direct choke and racing-type

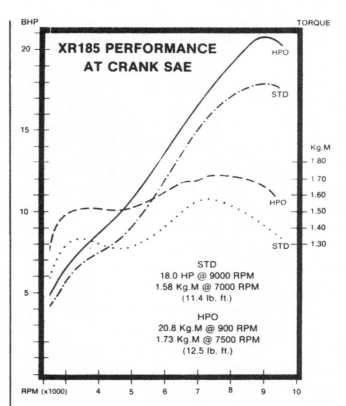

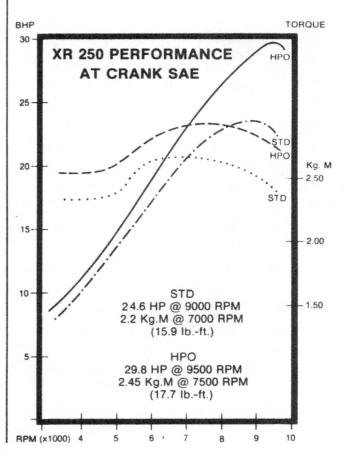

XR-185

Opposite: Knobby Shop offers partial and complete frame kits for XL and XR Hondas. This is their big-bore 450cc XL motocrosser with cantilever rear suspension using twin Fox AirShoxs. Front forks are Simons. Travel is 280mm at each end.

quick-turn throttle and cable. Kit also includes high capacity air inlets for the stock airbox.

Also included in the complete kit: optional 46 and 50-tooth rear sprockets. (standard sprocket has 48 teeth).

It is obvious from the descriptions of the kits that if you are building a high-performance enduro bike the complete kit for each bike is the best way to go. On the other hand, if you are building up a competitive motocross type bike it would be cheaper to get just the important sub-assemblies like piston kits, cylinder kits and cams. For an exhaust system you'll want to fabricate a lighter and better performing tuned megaphone design exhaust. And for the carburetor kit you'll want a Mikuni of appropriate size rather than a Kehin, since the Mikuni seems to carburate better in mid-range. And a Gunner Gasser throttle assembly and cable available from Moto-X Fox is popular for both enduro and motocross to prevent snagged cables.

Another company deeply involved in the modification of Honda four-stroke singles, particularly for motocross, is Knobby Shop International. The quality and performance of their English-built frame kits are exceptional, and they offer their own line of engine performance parts for the XR bikes along with a complete engine building service if you need it.

So in conclusion, look to your local Honda dealer for either a complete XR bike or XR engine, High Performance Options kits, and related parts for building up your ultimate four-stroke Honda weapon. Moto-X Fox can provide you with the best suspension parts and whatever accessories you might need to finish the bike. C&J Precision Products or Knobby Shop International has the frame kit you'll need to tie it all together.

C&J Precision Products, Inc.
1151 Mission Road
Fallbrook, California 92028
(714) 728-1707

Knobby Shop International
P.O. Box 1592
La Jolla, California 92038
(714) 452-1783

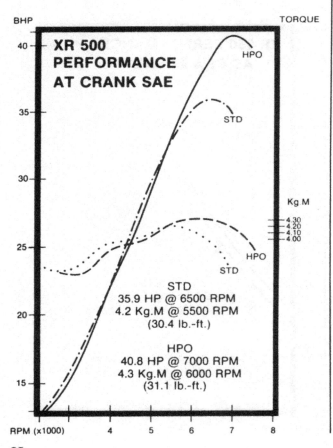

BHP TORQUE

XR 500 PERFORMANCE AT CRANK SAE

HPO
STD
Kg M
4.30
4.20
4.10
4.00
HPO
STD

STD
35.9 HP @ 6500 RPM
4.2 Kg.M @ 5500 RPM
(30.4 lb.-ft.)

HPO
40.8 HP @ 7000 RPM
4.3 Kg.M @ 6000 RPM
(31.1 lb.-ft.)

RPM (x1000)   4   5   6   7   8

Below: Team Honda's 1979 Enduro Team of Ray Plumb, Rick Munyon, Bob Nickelsen, Ted Worrell and Bill Bell.

HONDA PERFORMANCE PARTS FROM MOTO-X FOX

Below is a partial listing of the numerous performance parts, clothing, and accessories available from Moto-X Fox to fit Honda CR motocross bikes and XR Enduro bikes.

For information on parts ordering as well as any specific questions regarding bike preparation you can call Moto-X Fox during business hours at (408) 371-1221. The latest Moto-X Fox accessory catalog has a complete listing of competition parts and accessories and is available for $3.00 from Moto-X Fox, 520 McGlincy Lane, Campbell, CA 95008 USA.

99-1775 Fox Airshox 17.75" with negative spring	41-0012 Fox Works Handlebars, Honda
99-1750 Fox AirShox 17.50"	15-2040 Fox Shorty Levers, Honda
94-1001 Fox Factory Forks, Honda CR 250R	03-1000 Gunner Gasser Throttle
37-0219 Simons Forks, Honda CR-250R	Terrycables
Fox Factory Shocks	17-0044 Moto-X Fox Tank Stickers, CR-250R,R2
97-2003 Fox Factory Swingarm, CR-250R	17-0049 Moto-X Fox Tank Stickers, CR-125R
39-1025 Gas Fork Caps, CR-125R, CR-250R,R2	70-1051 Rear Sprocket, 49T, Honda CR-250R,R2
76-1009 Aluminum Muffler, CR-250R,R2	15-1052 Fork Skins, Honda CR-125R, CR-250R2
36-0003 Mikuni 36mm Carb, CR-250R	15-1046 Fork Skins, Honda CR-250R
62-2009 Poly-Air Filter, CR-250R,R2	45-2658 Fox Deluxe Seat Cover, Honda CR-250R,R2
62-2022 Poly-Air Filter, CR-125R	45-2667 Fox Deluxe Seat Cover, Honda CR-125R
Sun Rims, all models	73-0008 FIM Number Plates, Honda CR-250R,R2
Metzeler Dunlop Yokohama Tires	73-0010 FIM Number Plates, Honda CR-125R

PREPARING THE CR HONDA FOR COMPETITION

Steve Wise.

THE VARIABLE LEVERAGE RATIO SUSPENSION WORKS HONDAS

During the 1979 Trans-USA Series Team Honda debuted an all-new works bike which we could label as an RC 380-79 VLRS. As expected, the bike featured a new engine design with displacement reduced to 380cc for the Open class, making it much easier for the Factory riders to control than the somewhat excessive and explosive RC 450 engine which had been in use since 1978. The engine design of the 380cc is very small and compact and probably derived from the RC 250 to keep things as light as possible. In effect, an overbored 250cc motor which is undersquare in its bore/stroke ratio to allow it to be very responsive and quick revving, yet with enough displacement to offer a broad and tractable powerband.

Even more interesting than the new engine design the RC 380-79 featured variable leverage ratio rear suspension. The concept was not new, since Kawasaki's Uni-Trak bikes employ the same principle and VLRS shock mounting designs had been seen five years earlier, but Honda's application of the VLRS swingarm was the best and the most serious approach yet seen. Honda's VLRS swingarm design is also nice in that it can be used on conventional style motocross bike frames with standard type shock absorber units.

Steve Wise and the Honda RC 380-79 VLRS bike which he raced during the 1979 Trans-U.S.A. Series. This was a simple and effective way to experiment with VLRS before bringing out a completely new design bike which for the 1980 season would be the all-new monoshock Pro-Link.

The concept behind Honda's VLRS swingarm is as follows: by attaching the shocks to the swingarm by way of a bell crank which pivots on the swingarm and is also connected to the frame, the shock absorber unit's leverage ratio varies as the rear wheel and swingarm move. By varying the ratio from higher to lower as the suspension travels from full extension to full compression, dampening is softer for the smaller bumps usually encountered when the suspension is extended and firmer for the larger bumps usually encountered when the suspension becomes compressed. This is important because conventional shock absorber designs are only speed sensitive in their dampening characteristics and VLRS allows them to be position sensitive as well. VLRS applies to spring rates, too. Straight rate springs become progressive in action, while progressive rate springs become even more progressive in action.

At Anaheim Stadium, the final Supercross of the 1979 season, Team Honda introduced another all-new VLRS bike which would be used during the 1980 racing season and establish the direction of their future designs. Called the Pro-Link, Honda's

new RC works bike was indeed very similar to Kawasaki's trend setting Uni-Trak system with a single rear monoshock located in the frame just behind the engine and employing VLRS. Honda's Pro-Link offers some important differences when compared to Kawasaki's Uni-Trak, though, and shows that when Honda puts their mind to something they can improve a concept better than anything which has come before.

Once again, the whole idea of the Pro-Link is variable leverage ratio suspension. VLRS uses changing geometry in the rear suspension components to allow the shock absorber/spring assembly to work less when the rear suspension is in the area of full extension and to work more when the rear suspension travels towards full compression.

The operational result with VLRS is a very soft rear suspension when extended to offer good wheel control over small bumps which the suspension usually encounters in this position. Like the small bumps down a straightaway or chatter bumps encountered while braking into corners. While lots of compression of the rear suspension, such as off jumps or through deep whoops, reduces leverage on the shock/

A close-up of the VLRS swingarm linkage used with Kayaba deCarbon reservoir shocks.

Chuck Sun and the RC 250-80 watercooled Pro-Link at Anaheim.

spring assembly to increase dampening and spring rate to meet the additional loading force.

Just what kind of changes in leverage ratio does the Pro-Link Honda offer from full extension of the rear suspension to full compression? Well, a production Honda CR 250-80 with conventional swingarm and shock arrangement offers a leverage ratio of 2.3 to 1.9 (a 17% change) from extension to compression. As you can see just the proper location of the shock assembly in the standard swingarm rear suspension can offer a slight amount of VLRS during rear wheel travel. The VLRS swingarm which Honda introduced during the Trans-USA increased this leverage ratio change from 2.5 to 1.8 (a 28% change) from extension to compression, not a radical change over conventional Honda rear suspension, but significant none the less. Once Honda tested and proved these geometry changes with the VLRS swingarm bike, the Pro-Link was the next step in getting away from conventional shocks. The Pro-Link RC 250s offer a leverage ratio change in the 3.75 to 2.75 (a 27% change) range. The higher overall leverage ratio of the Pro-Link design is necessary because the Honda Showa monoshock is located closer to

the swingarm pivot and has a proportionally shorter shaft travel than a conventional type shock.

The Pro-Link offers many advantages over the VLRS swingarm of the RC 380-79 bike Honda introduced just two months earlier. One major improvement is that the Pro-Link has fewer working parts and less unsprung weight located on a shorter moment arm from the swingarm pivot. That translates to a smoother rear suspension with quicker response.

There are also two nice advantages in locating the Pro-Link's attachment points and shock assembly so close to the engine and the middle of the bike's chassis. The first is that by moving the bike's mass or weight closer to the center of gravity which is somewhere near the middle of the bike . . . probably near the area of the reed valve assembly and cylinder . . . the bike itself becomes much more responsive in handling. Directional changes, like in corners or over jumps, become much easier.

The other advantage in locating the rear suspension's input forces so close to the bike's center of gravity is improved weight transfer under acceleration and braking. There is more force available to

The Honda RC250-80 Watercoold Pro Link works bikes premiered both watercooling and a single shock rear suspension at the Anaheim Supercorss in January 1980. Behind the bike in the picture above are riders Chuck Sun and Donnie Hansen, with Honda tuner Cliff White talking to Fox Shox suspension engineer Steve Johnson..

a number of aftermarket accessory companies selling nothing but parts to make the CR 125M highly competitive. And of course there was Marty Smith......

Because of his National Championship in the 125cc class Marty was the only rider Honda retained for 1975 from their otherwise lackluster 1974 season. Joining Marty on the now much reduced Honda team was proven winner Pierre Karsmakers, along with two new backup rookies, Rich Eierstedt and Tommy Croft.

1975 was also the year that Honda proved it was serious about winning in American motocross. Not so much because it would help them sell more motocross bikes, because in that area they still felt the potential was limited, but because they felt the publicity and public relations from motocross was good for the Honda image in general. That's why for the next three years they would campaign National and World Championship events without a serious production motocrosser to sell.

The factory bikes Honda introduced in the spring of 1975 were completely changed, all new RC works bikes designed specifically for long suspension travel and painted the now famous Honda red. Only the RC 125-75 bared resemblence to the production CR 125M Elsinore with a similar looking engine. The RC 250-75 and RC 400-75 had their own unique engine

designs which proved to be ultimate in simplicity, function and light weight. Such inovations as adjustable outside ignition timing and rearward positioned transmission countershafts for more consistant drive chain tension with long travel suspension were pioneered in the first RCs. These bikes would later be known as the Type Is because of their nearly upright shock positioning on the swingarm compared to the RCs which would follow in 1976 with cantilever positioned rear shocks and be labeled the Type IIs.

There was a lot of secrecy concerning these bikes. The RC-125 had provision on its engine cases for the addition of what may have been a crankshaft fuel injection system. It was also known that the Open class RC was available in various engine capacities ranging from 360,380,400,420,460 and 480cc as the factory and riders experimented with various bore and stroke ratios and displacements.

Marty Smith proved to Honda they had made the right choice in keeping him on the team as he destroyed the 125cc National Championship for the second year in a row, winning every race but one in an expanded series which now included seven events.

Marty rode in other classes as well when the dates weren't conflicting to finish eight overall in both the 250cc National and 500cc National Champion-

Billy Grossi's RC 250-74 was outdated in the suspension department.

load the front or rear wheels under braking or acceleration to improve traction.

Honda's Pro-Link even offers a few design improvements over Kawasaki's Uni-Trak. Honda's leverage rocker arm system is lighter, sturdier and more protected than Kawasaki's. Spring preload, ride height and rear wheel travel are quickly and easily adjusted on the Honda from outside the bike. The Kawasaki requires partial disassembly to make adjustments for preload and offers no real provision for altering ride height or rear wheel travel.

Just as interesting as the new Pro-Link rear suspension is the watercooled RC 250 engine which appeared with the new bike. Not just a bolt-on kit, the watercooled RC 250-80 engine required almost a complete redesign over earlier Honda 250cc powerplants. The complete cooling system includes twin waterpumps driven off the crankshaft which circulate coolant through the head and cylinder assembly twice amid a tangle of hoses and cast magnesium pipes. Twin aluminum radiators are hung on each side of the frame near the bike's steering head and are hidden by ducted cowlings which work in conjunction with a ducted gas tank design to assist air flow through the radiators.

For the majority of Supercross races Honda will run the Pro-Link bikes without the watercooling systems, relying on aircooling to accomplish the job in the shorter stadium motos. Watercooling will be used at outdoor races with their longer 45-minute motos.

The Pro-Link system will certainly find its way to use on all displacement classes of RC works bikes during the 1980 racing season and could possibly be found on the 1981 CR production bikes.

The RC 125-80 works bikes should be running a watercoling system that is identical to the system used on the Mugen racing team bikes. Similar watercooling kits are available from Mugen to fit CR 125R-80 production bikes. The only difference in the kits is that they will use radiators which mount to the front fork triple clamps of the bike so the stock gas tank can be retained, allowing easier installation of the radiator without the need for a special hand-built aluminum tank.

Upper left: Team Mugen rider Johnny O'Mara in action on the Mugen ME 125 watercooled bike. Lower left: Texas Toronado Steve Wise (right) and ace tuner Paul Turner (left) with the RC 250-80 Pro-Link bike prepared for Supercross. These bikes use similar frame geometry to the 1978-79 CR 250R bikes, but with lengthened swingarm to gain a longer 59-60 inch wheelbase. 300mm suspension travel is used for both Supercross and the outdoor Nationals. With support from Moto-X Fox, Steve was the only privateer to ever win a National motocross, and now with Team Honda he still relies on Moto-X Fox riding gear exclusively. Right: A parts breakdown of the Honda/Mugen watercooled 125cc.

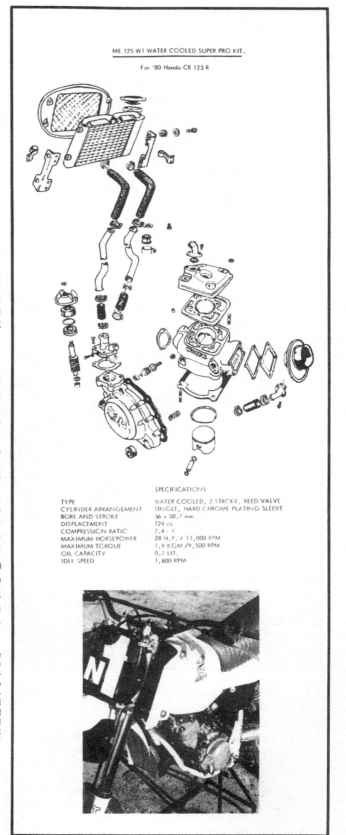

ME 125 W1 WATER COOLED SUPER PRO KIT.

For '80 Honda CR 125 R

SPECIFICATIONS

TYPE	WATER COOLED, 2 STROKE, REED VALVE
CYLINDER ARRANGEMENT	SINGLE, HARD CHROME PLATING SLEEVE
BORE AND STROKE	56 x 50.7 mm
DISPLACEMENT	124 cc
COMPRESSION RATIO	7.4 : 1
MAXIMUM HORSEPOWER	28 H.P. / 11,000 RPM
MAXIMUM TORQUE	1.9 KGM /9,500 RPM
OIL CAPACITY	0.7 LIT.
IDLE SPEED	1,800 RPM

Honda has made some significant changes to the 1980 model CR 125 and CR 250 production bikes. The most obvious changes to other models include twin front downtube frames, necessitating new engine cylinders with center-port exhaust exiting between the frame downtubes. Both bikes now have sturdier plastic tanks to replace the previous aluminum fuel tanks. There's now new Showa deCarbon reservoir shocks replacing the previous emulsion gas charged shocks. And gone are the "Saddleback Road Race Special" tires, replaced by much better Bridgestone motocross tires.

MODIFYING THE 1980 PRODUCTION BIKES

Lenny Giger.

The claims for the new twin front downtube frame, which is derived directly from the 1979 RC factory bikes, are that there is a substantial increase in chassis rigidity and a reduction in torsional flex with the new twin front downtube frame compared to the old single front downtube frame. This is somewhat questionable since there are many successful works and production motocrossers with single front downtube frames. Then with the introduction of the 1980 Pro-Link RC 250 works bikes we see Honda running frames with a single front downtube going

down from the steering, branching into a twin front downtube just in time to clear the center-port exhaust of the engine cylinder. Clearly, Honda is trying new engineering ideas and then putting them into production even if they offer no major improvement.

On the CR 250-80 the twin front downtube frame brings with it a significant increase in weight, close to five pounds. This one point alone makes it fairly attractive to race an older and less expensive 1978 or 1979 model CR 250R, particularly if you plan to

HONDA CR 125R-80

SPECIFICATIONS:

IMPORTER: American Honda Motor Co.
100 West Alondra Blvd.
Gardena, California 90247

CATEGORY: motocross

SUGGESTED RETAIL PRICE: $1329

ENGINE
Type	two-stroke vertical single
Port arrangement	one reed-valve-controlled intake, four transfers, one booster transfer, one exhaust
Bore and stroke	55.5mm x 50.7mm
Displacement	122.7cc
Compression ratio (corrected)	8.0:1
Carburetion	one 34mm Keihin slide / needle
Air filter	two-stage washable oiled foam element
Lubrication	pre-mixed fuel and oil
Starting system	primary kick
Ignition	internal-rotor magneto CDI
Charging system	none

DRIVETRAIN
Primary drive	straight-cut gears
Primary drive ratio	3.158:1
Clutch	wet, multi-plate
Final drive type	#520 chain (⅜-in. pitch, ¼-in. width)
Final drive	13/51: 3.92:1

Gear	Internal gear ratio	Overall gear ratio	MPH per 1000 RPM
I	2.54	31.44	2.4
II	1.87	23.23	3.3
III	1.56	19.28	4.0
IV	1.30	16.11	4.8
V	1.14	14.07	5.5
VI	1.00	12.39	6.2

DIMENSIONS AND CAPACITIES
Weight	202 lbs. (91.6kg)
Weight distribution	45.8% front, 54.2% rear
Wheelbase	54.8 to 55.6 in. (139.2 to 141.2cm)
Seat height	36.8 in. (935mm)
Handlebar width	33.5 in. (851mm)
Footpeg height	15.6 in. (396mm)
Ground clearance	13.0 in. (330mm), at frame cradle
Steering head angle	28.3 degrees from vertical
Front wheel trail	4.53 in. (115mm)
Frame	tubular chromoly steel, double front downtubes
Fuel tank	plastic, 1.7 gal. (6.5l), no reserve
Instrumentation	none

PERFORMANCE
Top speed (calculated)	68 mph (109 kph)

All weights and measurements are taken with machine unladen and fuel tank empty.

SUSPENSION/WHEEL TRAVEL, IN.
Front	air / spring, 37mm stanchion tube diameter / 11.5 in. (292mm)
Rear	5-way adj. spring preload, 2-way adj. rebound damping / 10.8 in. (275mm)

BRAKES
Front	drum, single-leading shoe
Rear	drum, single-leading shoe, rod-operated

TIRES
Front	3.00-21 Bridgestone Motocross M23
Rear	4.00-18 Bridgestone Motocross M22

PERFORMANCE:

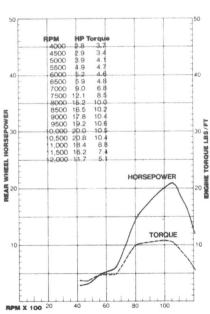

RPM	HP	Torque
4000	2.8	3.7
4500	2.9	3.4
5000	3.9	4.1
5500	4.9	4.7
6000	5.2	4.6
6500	5.9	4.8
7000	9.0	6.8
7500	12.1	8.5
8000	15.2	10.0
8500	16.5	10.2
9000	17.8	10.4
9500	19.2	10.6
10,000	20.0	10.5
10,500	20.8	10.4
11,000	18.4	8.8
11,500	16.2	7.4
12,000	11.7	5.1

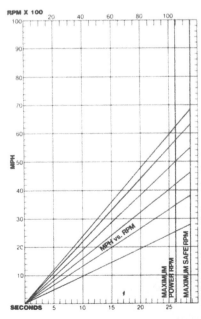

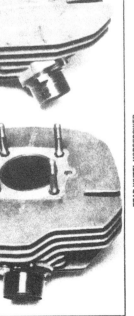

New downtube-clearing center-port cylinder

More finning for improved cooling, cast-iron liner for easier repair.

HONDA CR 250R-80

Suggested retail price...N.A.
Warranty..None
Number of U.S. dealers...1787
Cost of shop manual.......................................Included

ENGINE

Type.......................Two-stroke reed-valve single
Displacement..247cc
Bore x stroke.............................70 x 64.4mm
Compression..7.3:1
Carburetion..............1, 36mm Keihin slide needle
Ignition..CDI
Lubrication...Premix
Air filter...Oiled foam

DRIVETRAIN

Primary transmission...............Straight-cut gears, 3.25:1
Clutch..7 plates, wet
Final drive..............⅝ x ¼ (No. 520) D.I.D. chain, 49/14

CHASSIS

Fork................Showa, 37mm, air/spring, 11.8 in. travel
Shocks..................Showa, gas/oil, 11.4 in. wheel travel
Front tire................3.00-21 Bridgestone Motocross M17
Rear tire................5.10-18 Bridgestone Motocross M20
Rake/trail..........................28.5°/4.5 in. (114mm)
Wheelbase..................................57.38 in. (1457mm)
Seat height...............................38.25 in. (971mm)
Ground clearance.....................13.38 in. (339mm)
Fuel capacity.....................2.2 gal. (8.5 liters)
Wet weight............................237 lbs. (107kg)
Colors..Red

PERFORMANCE

Power to weight ratio.....................................8.2 lbs./hp
RPM at 60 mph in top gear.............................7300 rpm
Speed in gears at (redline)............(6500) 1st 23.58 mph;
          2nd 28.15 mph; 3rd 36.13 mph;
          4th 44.79 mph; 5th 53.38 mph

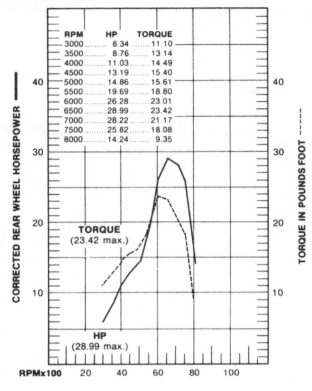

RPM	HP	TORQUE
3000	6.34	11.10
3500	8.76	13.14
4000	11.03	14.49
4500	13.19	15.40
5000	14.86	15.61
5500	19.69	18.80
6000	26.28	23.01
6500	28.99	23.42
7000	28.22	21.17
7500	25.82	18.08
8000	14.24	9.35

TORQUE
(23.42 max.)

HP
(28.99 max.)

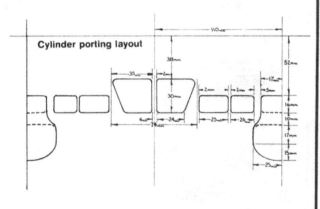

Cylinder porting layout

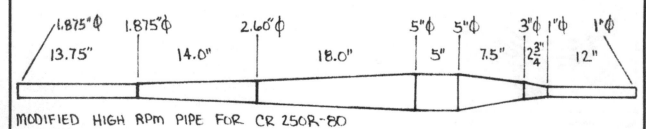

1.875"∅   1.875"∅   2.60"∅   5"∅   5"∅   3"∅ 1"∅   1"∅
13.75"   14.0"   18.0"   5"   7.5" 2¾"   12"

MODIFIED HIGH RPM PIPE FOR CR 250R-80

make modifications to the suspension and engine anyway. Along with the weight of the new frame on the CR 250R-80, there are a few more pounds in the new reservoir Showa shocks and the one inch longer steel swingarm which increase rear wheel travel from 280mm to 290mm. Front fork travel remains the same at 300mm, but with the fork spring rate now provided some adjustability with air caps.

It is in the CR 125-80 that major improvements are found, both in the handling and in the engine. Gone is the ill-handling 23-inch front wheel assembly of the past year, replaced by the more standard 21-inch front wheel assembly with changes in the geometry of the new twin front downtube frame to suit. The result is that the 1980 model CR 125 is a much better handling bike than the 1979 model. There has also been a slight increase in peak engine horsepower with the new center-port cylinder bike over the previous year's model.

SUSPENSION MODIFICATIONS

The 1980 model CR 125 and CR 250 Hondas remain excellent and competitive production bikes, but as in the past there are major shortcomings with the stock suspension, particularly for a Pro level rider. It is with the suspension we suggest you begin any modifications whatsoever before looking to improve the performance of the engine. A faster motor will do you no good if your bike doesn't handle right, and in fact will probably worsen the bikes's performance on the track, while a better handling bike in itself will help the rider to go faster with less fatigue.

There are two companies deeply involved in improving the handling and performance of Honda CRs. The first is, of course, Moto-X Fox. The engineers at Moto-X Fox have worked closely with their own team riders (Larry Wosick, Lenny Giger, JoJo Keller, Jim Turner and Carlos Serrano) as well as American Honda and its team riders in the development and testing of the latest Fox Factory suspension components for Hondas. The goal was to offer to the public suspension components that are the finest in the world, equal or better in performance to what even the factory teams have supplied to them from their own engineers.

Then there is Mugen, owned by Hirotoshi Honda, with direct links to the Honda factory in Japan. Mugen's concern is the selling and manufacturing of limited production Honda racing parts, or even complete bikes. Many of the parts offered by them are the same as those being used on the latest RC factory Hondas, or are performance hop-up items designed specifically for CR production Hondas, but engineered and manufactured with the same quality as RC factory parts.

The first place to begin improving the Honda's suspension is with replacement of the rear shocks. The latest aluminum bodied Showa reservoir shocks are what the factory Honda team ran with during some events in 1979, but they never worked for them and don't work well on the production bikes. The best shock to replace them with is the new Fox Factory Shock, available with either remote or piggyback reservoirs. These shocks are guaranteed not to fade, extremely rugged, easily worked on in minutes with simply a screwdriver and an adjustable wrench, and offer more tuning variables than any other shock on the market. There are separate and tunable high and low speed rebound and compression dampening circuits and a wide choice of dual springs, straight rate and progressive. Fox Factory Shocks are available in lengths of 16.00 ins. for CR 125R-80s with stock or Mugen swingarms; 17.0 ins. for CR 125R-79s with stock or Mugen swingarms and CR 250R-78 thru 80s with stock, Mugen or Fox Factory Swingarms, for approximately 280mm of standard rear wheel travel; and 17.5 ins. for CR 250-78 thru 80s with stock, Mugen or Fox Factory, for approximately 300-320mm of rear wheel travel.

Fox AirShoxs are also available and provide the benefit of easily adjustable air springs. AirShox are available in 16¼", 16¾", 17", and 17¾" lengths, but they will not fit on stock CR 125R-80 swingarms. There may also be a slight interference fit with AirShoxs on the mounting brackets of Mugen swingarms, but this is easily corrected with a little filing or grinding for clearance on the brackets.

Both Fox Factory and Mugen offer excellent box-section aluminum swingarms for CR Hondas which reduce weight over the stock steel swingarms and provide a worthwhile increase in strength and rigidity. Both Fox Factory and Mugen swingarms come complete with all parts necessary for installation. Fox Factory Swingarms are only available for CR-250R bikes, while Mugen swingarms are available for both CR-125R and CR-250R bikes. The Fox Factory and Mugen swingarms are the same length as the stock CR 250R-80 steel swingarm, which is one inch longer than the stock CR 250R-78 and -79 model swingarms. Using stock length 17.0 inch shocks with the Fox Factory and Mugen swingarm on all model CR 250Rs will yield approximately 280mm of rear wheel travel, while 17.5 inch shocks will yield approximately 300mm of rear wheel travel.

The CR 250-80 production bike's chassis and frame geometry is a direct copy of the prototype RC 250-79 twin front downtube bike which Steve Wise raced in the Supercross Series and Nationals. This bike geometry featured a shorter frame design, resulting in a reduction in the distance from the front wheel axle to swingarm pivot, 37 inches to 35.5 inches or a decrease in 1.5 inches total, over previous CR 250Rs and RC works bikes. To compensate for the loss in overall wheelbase length, Honda used a 1.0 inch longer swingarm on the RC 250-79 and CR 250-80 to return the wheelbase to approximately 57.5 inches. This chassis geometry will work well on smoother Supercross type tracks or with shorter

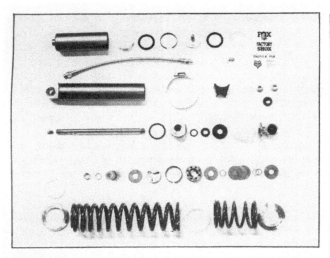

Here's a breakdown of the parts making up a Fox Factory Shock employing remote reservoir. Ruggedly designed and easily rebuildable, they offer a complete range of adjustability in both dampening and spring rates, with performance better than any other shock on the market at this time.

280mm (11.0 ins.) suspension travel. On high-speed or rough motocross tracks there can be stability problems with this short of a wheelbase.

A Fox Factory Swingarm used in conjunction with a CR 250R-78 or 79 single-front downtube frame provides a much better handling bike with a much more stable 59.0 inch wheelbase. As a matter of fact, the RC 250-80 Pro-Link works bikes return to the older CR/RC single-front downtube frame geometry specifications and a longer swingarm to get a 59.0 inch wheelbase. The RC 250-80 Pro-Link bike runs 295mm (11.8 ins.) of suspension travel. If you are running a CR 250-80 frame with 300mm (12.0 ins.) of travel it is suggested you use a Fox Factory Swingarm with the rear wheel adjusted in the most rearward position to gain a 58.0 inch wheelbase. Team Moto-X Fox is in the process of testing an even longer swingarm with the CR 250-80 frame to gain a 59-60.0 inch wheelbase and will release it if it proves successful.

Once the problems at the rear end of the CR Hondas have been corrected, attention can next be turned to the front forks. Here, two major modifica-

For the 1980 racing season, the factory teams from Yamaha, Suzuki and Kawasaki have moved up to 43mm forks, but Fox Factory Forks at 44mm with their forged sliders and triple clamps continue to offer more strength and rigidity along with performance and adjustability to match. They offer a significant improvement over stock CR forks which are only 37mm and RC forks which are 39mm. Different rate springs, dampening rod rates, and amounts of front wheel travel are available.

tions are available from Mugen and Fox Factory.

The least expensive solution is available from Mugen. They offer 39mm Showa factory fork leg assemblies which come stock. Travel is increased to a full 300mm with these legs which incorporate air/coil springs and much more sophisticated dampening, similar to what is used on the RC factory Hondas. These forks use the stock CR front wheel axle and triple clamps, and the clamp holes in the CR triple clamps have to be rebored from 37mm to 39mm to fit. Most local machine shops should be able to perform this job easily.

The ultimate solution to improve the front suspension on CR Hondas is a set of Fox Factory Forks. With their forged triple clamps and slider legs, huge 44mm tubes, these are the strongest and most flex-free forks ever built. These also have air/coil springs for fine tuning-in of spring rates, while even more noticeable changes can be made with the optional softer or firmer dampening rods available and different springs. Different length dampening rods allow a choice of front wheel travel of either 305mm, or 330mm.

Team Moto-X Fox rider Lenny Giger in action on the Fox prepared CR 250R-80 production bike. For Supercross races the bikes are set up with 11 inches of travel to aid maneuverability on tight courses.

Fox Factory's swingarm for CR 250R Hondas is welded up in box-section of aircraft quality aluminum then heat-treated to T-6 to offer the utmost in strength and reliability. Note the aluminum plate chain guide. Shocks are Fox Factory with piggyback reservoirs.

ENGINE MODIFICATIONS

Because of its relationship with the Honda factory which allows it access to factory tuning information and limited production ME parts, Mugen is the best choice for parts when it comes to improving the engine performance of CR models. Mugen will sell parts individually, as complete kits, and even completely modified bikes if desired.

The ME 125cc engine kits from Mugen offer a substantial power increase over stock CRs, at a slight sacrifice to tractability and low-end power. Complete watercooling kits are also available and claimed to be even lighter when fully assembled on the bike than just the aircooled kits, thanks to lightweight pump parts, thin cylinder and head castings, and the aluminum radiator. The watercooled kits are the same as the crankshaft driven pump watercooling kits as used on the factory RC and Mugen ME race bikes, but with the radiator mounted to the fork triple clamps rather than either side of the frame steering head to reduce the cost of the special ducted gas tank which is otherwise needed. Mugen also expects to offer complete watercooled ME 125 W1 bikes assembled in America by November 1980, complete with the best possible suspension components. No complete aircooled bikes are offered, just the kits.

Mugen offers an ME 250 kit for CRs consisting of a new cylinder, special piston assembly, and exhaust pipe. The standard CR 250R-80 cylinder is an exact copy of what Team Honda ran on their RCs during the 1979 season and proved to be very competitive, but many Pro riders feel they need more power still. American Honda's team mechanics claim there is a substantial increase in power, close to 8 horsepower, available with just a properly redesigned exhaust pipe. No such exhaust pipes or specifications are available for them at this time, so it is suggested that the stock CR cylinder be used in conjunction with a Mugen ME exhaust pipe. The CR stock piston on all model CR 250Rs using unbridged rear intake/transfer ports ('78 and '80 cylinders) can be modified with a port window near the top of the intake skirt to help feed the rear transfer port from the crankcase.

If you want to race an Open class CR Honda the only way to go is Mugen's ME 360 kit which converts a CR 250R engine with some machine work into a 360cc Open class bike. The bike won't win too many drag races against other larger displacement bikes, but once out on a track the Mugen 360cc kit is highly competitive. The rider has a snappy, quick revving powerband at his disposal like a 250cc bike, but with a much broader and stronger powerband. Honda's Steve Wise raced a somewhat similar 380cc RC Honda engine in the 1979 Trans-USA Series, while Marty Smith raced a 360cc Mugen engined bike in the 1979 AMA 500cc Nationals.

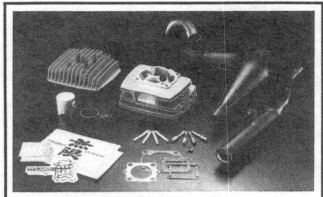

The components in a typical Mugen engine kit.

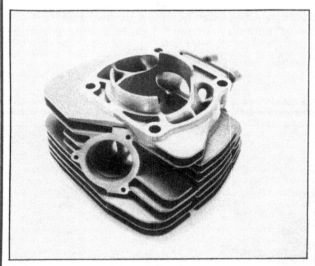

A Mugen chrome cylinder for the 360cc kit.

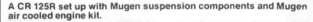

A CR 125R set up with Mugen suspension components and Mugen air cooled engine kit.

The complete Mugen ME 125 W1 watercooled bike for the ultimate125cc class terror. Watercooling kits from Mugen used a fork mounted radiator for use with the stock gas tank, crank driven water pump. This is Johnny O'Mara's bike raced in the 1980/81 California Winter Series tuned by Al Baker.

PREPARING THE CR HONDA FOR COMPETITION

1980 PRICE LIST AND INFORMATION

FOX FACTORY SHOCKS, complete with dual springs and either remote or piggyback reservoirs. All lengths available.	$275-295.00
FOX FACTORY AIRSHOXS, complete. Dual-stage adjustable air springs. All lengths, and 99-1775 with negative spring.	295.00
FOX FACTORY SWINGARM, complete. Fits CR 250R models only.	235.00
FOX FACTORY FORKS, complete with different tuning for either CR 125Rs or CR 250Rs. Lengths of travel either 11, 12 or 13 inches. Optional springs and dampening.	469.00
MUGEN SWINGARM, complete. Fits all CR 250/360 models.	250.00
MUGEN SWINGARM, complete. Fits CR 125R-79 model.	250.00
MUGEN SWINGARM, complete. Fits CR 125R-80 model.	250.00
MUGEN SHOWA FORKS, incomplete. 300mm (12 inch) travel. requires remachining of stock triple clamps and use of other stock parts.	250.00
MUGEN ME 125 ENGINE KIT, complete with cylinder, head, piston assembly, gaskets and bolts. Fits CR 125R-80 model only.	450.00
MUGEN ME 125 WATERCOOLED ENGINE KIT, complete with pump, primary cover, head, cylinder, piston assembly, radiator, all plumbing, and front number plate.	750.00
MUGEN ME 125 W1 WATERCOOLED BIKE, complete with watercooled engine kit, Mugen/Showa/Ohlins suspension. Production available for delivery about Nov. 1980. Deposit of $1,000.00 required by Sept. 1st, 1980.	3,000.00
MUGEN ME 250 ENGINE KIT, complete with exhaust pipe, $130.00; cylinder, $210.00; and piston assembly, $50.00	390.00
MUGEN ME 360 ENGINE KIT, complete with pipe, cylinder head, piston assembly, gaskets, bolts and fittings. Specify either CR 250R-78, 79 or CR 250R model frame.	650.00
MUGEN ME 360 ENGINE CASE MACHINING AND CRANK REBALANCING. Send stock engine cases and crank by mail or U.P.S.	150.00
MUGEN ME 360 ENGINE CASE MACHINING, CRANK BALANCING AND ASSEMBLY. Add cost of ME 360 kit and replacement of any worn stock parts. Ship by truck lines.	200.00
MUGEN ME 360 COMPLETE BIKE. With ME 360 kit and Mugen/Showa/Ohlins suspension. Allow 2-4 weeks delivery.	3,700.00

MOTO-X FOX, 520 McGlincey Lane, Campbell, California 95008 U.S.A., phone (408) 371-1221.
MUGEN U.S.A., 6878 Santa Fe Avenue East, Hesperia, California 92345 U.S.A., phone (714) 244-6405.

RC125 80 Twin Cylinder

     Here are photographs of one of the rarest, most exotic motocross bikes of all time, a factory Honda RC 125cc Twin Cylinder bike. There isn't much information about this machine, as it was never raced in America. I'm guessing it is a 1980/81 model year bike based on its similar construction in the frame, swingarm, and Pro-Link single rear shock suspension and similar components like the drum brakes and bodywork as seen on the other 1980 season Honda RC Pro-Link factory bikes.

     Where this bike obviously differs, is it is the only known 125cc 2-stroke twin cylinder and watercooled bike that Honda ever built. And it uses an exotic billet machined aluminum Ribi-style leading link front suspension incorporating a full-floating front brake and anti-dive.

     Of course, we've since learned that full floating brakes aren't really necessary on sport motorcycles, be it on dirt or pavement. Nor is an anti-dive front suspension,

since we want the front suspension to compress under braking to quicken up the steering angle going into a corner. Whereas the Ribi style front fork design was too complicated, heavy and maintenance intensive and damage prone compared to a conventional sliding tube front fork.

     The advantage of building a twin-cylinder motocross engine for a 125cc bike is that you can get significantly more horsepower (albeit at higher RPM) compared to a less powerful single cylinder engine in a class where peak horsepower is much more important than torque. I think I remember Honda racing this bike in the 125cc Motocross World Championship that one year where it won handily, after which twin cylinder engines were banned by the FIM as being too expensive. Although today, Aprilia has been racing its production 450cc Twin in the FIM Motocross Open Class.

On the next page is a test rider on the RC125 twin cylinder bike who looks a lot like Johnny O'Mara.

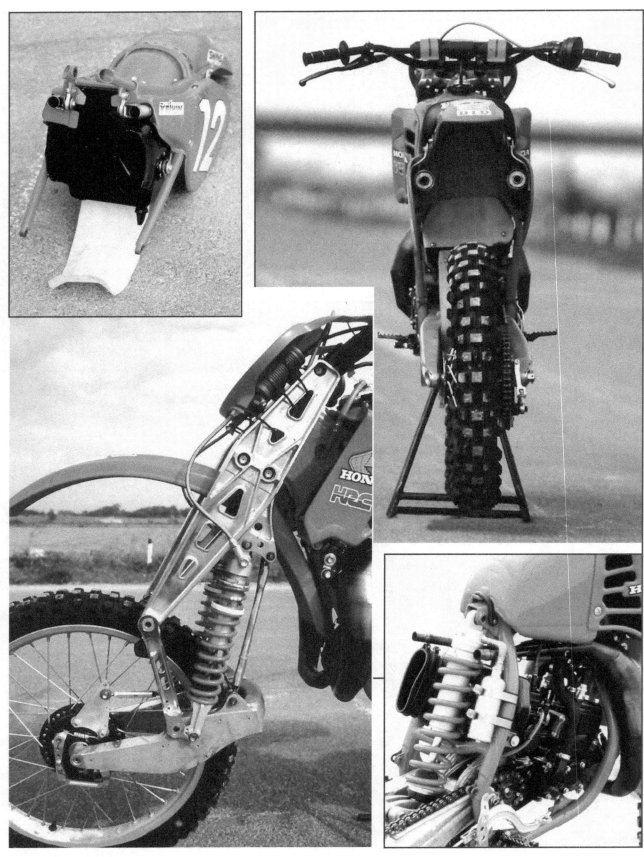

RC 125, 250 & 450 80 Pro-Link

Above:This is Steve Wise's new watercooled bike introduced at the 1980 AMA 250cc Outdoor Nationals. Compare it to the RC 250-80 air cooled bike shown on page 70 which Steve raced in Supercross just a few months earlier. Walking behind the front fender is Honda team rider Jim Gibson. Below: The aircooled RC 450-80 had more than enough power to not run at full throttle and to not need watercooling. Contemporary production 4-stoke motocross bikes some 30 years later weigh some 30 lbs. more and have far less power.

RC 125-80 Watercooled

Here is Honda's all new RC125 Pro-Link watercooled single cylsinder bike at the AMA Outdoor 1980 Nationals in the hands of factroy rider Rick Coon.

CPSIA information can be obtained
at www.ICGtesting.com
Printed in the USA
BVHW022314150223
658635BV00007B/141

9 781578 650989